Figuring Things Out

A Practical Guide to Critical Thinking
Fifth Edition

William J. Frayer
Central Maine Community College

KENDALL/HUNT PUBLISHING COMPANY
4050 Westmark Drive   Dubuque, Iowa 52002

For Pixie, Eric, Wendy, and Cassie

Contents

PREFACE

This book has been produced from material I have developed teaching critical thinking at Central Maine Community College since 1989. I remember well returning from the Sixth International Conference on Critical Thinking and Educational Reform at Sonoma State University in 1988, convinced that critical thinking was an essential and timely topic. It has occupied a prominent place in my life ever since, and this text is an outgrowth of that.

Although this is intended to be used as the essential elements of a critical thinking course, it can and should be supplemented with examples from the world around us: life experiences, op-ed pieces, advertisements, televised news events and debates, educational videos, and anything else that requires us to think and evaluate the world around us.

Chapters 1 through 3 provide the essential explanation of what critical thinking is. I have often used this material when presenting brief workshops for business and government employees. Chapters 4 through 7 develop the skills necessary to understand and critique real-world arguments. And finally, chapters 8 and 9 focus on the role of critical thinking in evaluating advertising and the news media. The appendix includes a suggested format for preparing commentaries on arguments and provides sample arguments.

I would like to thank my three children who each helped in various ways. Eric provided the artwork for the ad on page 119. Cassie provided the artwork for the ads on pages 118 and 120. Wendy designed the covers for the third and fourth editions. They all, along with my wife of over thirty years, Pixie, have encouraged me in all my projects, for which I am very grateful. I would also like to thank my students at Central Maine Community College who have, over the years, provided a considerable amount of honest feedback for me!

CHAPTER 1
What Is Critical Thinking?

Critical Thinking: Being Able to Figure Things Out

Susan is graduating from a technical college in May. It is now time for her to start looking for a job. She has the opportunity to keep her present part-time job which is related to her field of study and will likely turn into a full-time position. She is also considering looking for a job in a city about fifty miles away, where her boyfriend is working. Her instructor has told her about a job in another state with excellent opportunities for advancement.

John and his wife, Beth, are both working at jobs they enjoy, but they are considering when to start a family. Beth is twenty-nine and feels she should probably have a baby soon, but she enjoys her work and has an opportunity for a new position. They are worried that they will need a new house, and they are wondering if this is the best time to sell their home.

Sam runs a small building contracting business. His partner, Joel, has just learned of an opportunity to purchase some land. Joel is in favor of buying the land, subdividing it, and building speculative homes to sell. Sam is reluctant because the project involves borrowing a large sum of money. The risk is high, but so is the potential for a large profit.

In each of these situations, Susan, John and Beth, and Sam face difficult choices. They are complicated and require consideration of a number of important factors, some of which are unknowable: Will Susan stay with her boyfriend? Will Beth's pregnancy be difficult? Will the houses sell? Nevertheless, in each case, a decision has to be made in spite of such incomplete information.

Critical thinking provides us with the tools we need to be able to make difficult choices. Some people make these choices wisely; others do not. The difference is often in our ability to think through the problem carefully. Critical thinking helps us do this. It is a practical set of skills that can help us figure things out.

Children as Critical Thinkers

Babies know nothing about their environment when they arrive. They use their developing minds to gather the information they need to figure it all out. They quickly learn to apply the taste test to every small object to determine if it is food. They have a natural inclination to disassemble things to find out what they're made of. They crawl into every imaginable space to find out what's in there. They try out a variety of behaviors to determine what is, and is not, acceptable to their parents. Once they start to talk, they ask questions, incessantly, all day long. These activities enable them to make sense of their world by collecting and analyzing a huge amount of information in a small period of time. Children are natural-born critical thinkers. Unfortunately, children are not permitted to continue to behave in such an "undisciplined" manner for long. Beginning around age five, or often younger, children are introduced to school which, to varying degrees, requires conformity and organized learning. Often, children are not given the opportunity to continue to behave as natural learners but are forced to learn in a more organized way. This is accompanied by learning what is acceptable behavior as well. They learn to be quiet and not ask questions whenever they like. They must study what adults decide they should learn and are told when, and how, to learn it. They are trained to value the social rules of the classroom. Educators have debated for decades the controversy surrounding this transformation of the child from a natural learner to a disciplined student. Nevertheless, such a change does occur. It can be argued that when children are told what to think, they lose the ability to think for themselves. By the time American children reach high school, many of them cannot reason or communicate clearly.

Adults as Uncritical Thinkers

By the time we grow up, however, we are expected to know how to think for ourselves. The demands of our jobs, citizenship, and parenting all require us to be able to reason well. Unfortunately, many adults have learned to avoid thinking. They make decisions without getting all the pertinent facts. They jump to conclusions based on insufficient evidence. They react emotionally rather than rationally, later wishing they had thought about the situation more carefully. Because they never learned how to think in school, they are not able to reason well as adults.

Thinking is hard work, and we are expected to do it frequently. We have to figure out whether a certain used car would be a wise purchase. We have to figure out who to vote for. We have to figure out what we need to do to get a job that will pay well and that we will enjoy. We have to raise children and learn to live with our spouses. Each of these activities requires complex thinking that takes time and demands a considerable amount of mental energy. As a result, many of us don't invest the necessary effort to think clearly. We make bad decisions when we buy cars. We elect poor candidates to office. We end up in jobs that we dislike and which don't meet our needs. We suffer from a high divorce rate. It is often **easier** not to think. Not thinking takes less time and sometimes works. Usually, however, it doesn't work, and we pay a price for it.

This book is about learning to think better. It's based on the idea that thinking is a set of skills that we can learn and practice. As adults, we have learned other methods, besides thinking, for solving our problems and making decisions. Such non-thinking methods may include using our gut reaction or intuition, using our feelings or emotions, or just plain guessing. These methods often take less time but generally are not as reliable as using reasoning skills. It may be useful to consult our intuition, as long as we supplement it with critical thinking. We should also consider our feelings, as long as we don't ignore the evidence. Before we learn to think better, we need to clearly understand what it means to be able to think well and how thinking differs from intuition and emotions. In a sense, we have to unlearn bad habits as we develop good ones.

Thinking versus Feeling

One of the most common problems we need to address immediately is our tendency to confuse thinking and feeling. We may understand the difference between these two words, but we often blur this distinction in practice. Thinking involves using the left, logical side of the brain to sort out evidence and reach a conclusion by applying that evidence in a reasonable manner. Feeling, in contrast, involves our involuntary reaction to emotional stimuli to produce anger, fear, happiness, or sadness. We may be able to learn to control the way we react to our feelings, but we often cannot control the feelings themselves. When we are faced with a decision, we often experience thoughts and feelings simultaneously. As critical thinkers, we need to be able to understand our feelings and not to allow them to dominate our behavior.

Obviously, we need to be able to think **and** feel to be a fully functioning person. On one hand, we need to develop our rational side so we can make good choices about our jobs, our money, and other issues that involve analyzing and comparing data. At the same time, we are living with our emotions as well. We feel love for those around us; we are afraid of things we don't understand; and we are sad when we suffer losses. In fact, many decisions require that we consider both our emotions and our thoughts. When we decide to change jobs, get married, or take a vacation, we need to consider both. Sometimes our feelings will conflict with our better judgment. We may not want to take a new job because we are fearful of the change, but when we use our logic, we understand that it may be for the best. We all know the feeling of wanting to buy a car that probably wouldn't be reliable, just because we were carried away by our emotions. Sometimes we listen to our hearts instead of our heads anyway. Sometimes this is the right thing to do, but not usually. Relying exclusively on our emotions often leads to undesirable consequences.

The problem is that since we don't practice thinking regularly, we often let our emotions take over, which blurs our judgment. When we are faced with an important decision, we sometimes do not acknowledge our feelings and keep them under control. This, more often than not, results in confusion between our rational and emotional impulses. If we are not aware of what's happening, we can easily let our feelings take over.   When we discipline our children, we may let our anger decide how we respond rather than think the situation through logically. When we buy a car, we sometimes avoid the complexity of checking out the vehicle carefully because we want to buy it, and we don't want to wait. We may blow up at a coworker rather than take the time and effort to discuss our differences rationally. In each of these cases, if we had taken the time to think things through, we might have behaved differently.

We even confuse thinking with feeling in our language. We sometimes use the two words interchangeably. One manager might ask another how he "feels" about her proposal.   What she usually means is, what does he "think" about it. The words "think" and "feel" have two entirely different meanings. Critical thinking involves the use of our rational side. Most of us don't need to practice feeling; it comes naturally.

We may have trouble expressing or dealing with our feelings, but they usually make themselves known without having to practice. Thinking, on the other hand, requires considerable practice and attention if we are going to do it well. So when we study critical thinking, we are working to develop the logical side of our minds. This is not to suggest that feelings are not an important part of who we are. However thinking does not come as naturally and, therefore, requires a concentrated effort.

Recently, more research has been conducted concerning the role of emotions in effective decision making. In *Emotional Intelligence*, Daniel Goldman (1995, Bantam Books) argues that there are, in fact, emotional "skills" which we can develop, just as we can develop rational skills. This is an interesting area for further research. It is possible that such emotional skills as impulse control, persistence, and empathy may complement critical thinking skills. But these topics are beyond the scope of this text.

The Existence of Truth versus the Perception of Truth

The purpose of thinking clearly and carefully about something is to arrive at the truth about it. That is the purpose of critical thinking: to get to the truth. It is usually the best way to find the truth because it is the most reliable.

But what do we mean by truth? After all, what may be true to one person may not be true to another, so how can we be sure that a truth actually exists? How do we know that the truth is not a relative idea that exists differently in each person's mind?

The truth, in fact, can and does exist in many cases. We may not know what it is, but it exists just the same. Imagine that someone has been murdered. The police arrive to find the victim lying, face down, on the living room rug with a knife in his back. The police do not know how the knife came to be inserted in the man's back, but there **does** exist a truth about how it got there. We may never know how it got there, but the fact is, it did get there somehow. Exactly what happened, in this case, is the **truth** about it. The fact that we may not know what the truth is does not mean that it doesn't exist. It exists independently of our knowing it.

Consider the figure below. Although we may collect a large amount of information, or evidence, about how the crime occurred, we may not **know** the truth. A gap exists between the actual truth and what we know to be true.

TRUTH (How the knife actually ended up in the victim's back)

↑ What we KNOW. (The evidence we have from all sources, which reveals all we know about the truth. We arrive at this point by using critical thinking.)

Let's look at another example. Assume a woman wants to buy a car. She visits an auto dealer and finds a car she likes. Now she has to decide whether to buy it or not. Her previous two vehicles have been disasters. Both had serious mechanical problems that cost he a considerable amount of money. She is determined to avoid making the same mistake again, so she takes the car to her mechanic to check it out. She looks up the model in *Consumer Reports* to check its reliability. She wants to find out the truth about whether this vehicle will be reliable and inexpensive for her to maintain. She uses critical thinking skills to determine this truth by collecting and examining the evidence. Although the information she gets from the mechanic and the *Consumer Reports* is valuable, she won't know the absolute truth about the reliability of this vehicle until she owns it and runs it for a period of time. She can, however, increase her chances that she will get as close as possible to the truth. Using critical thinking will help her make a good decision by increasing the likelihood that she will find the truth. The truth about this vehicle does exist, whether she knows it or not.

Does there exist a truth for every question? No. Some questions have no truth. Whether chocolate ice cream is better than vanilla or whether a particular painting is more beautiful than another are questions that obviously have no objective truth. We could argue endlessly about them, applying our best critical thinking skills, and still not find a truth because for these types of questions, truth does not exist, except for each individual. We might call such questions **matters of preference**. Issues of taste or preference have no independent truth. There would, of course, be a truth about the ingredients of each type of ice cream, just as there would be a truth about the relative value of each painting on the art market. There would not, however, be a truth about which ice cream flavor tastes better, or which painting is more beautiful. It is up to the individual.

So, for what kinds of questions does there exist a truth? Any question which is not a matter of preference but a matter of fact, has a truth which can be sought. We may not ever arrive at the truth, but it can be sought. For example, whether it will rain tomorrow is a matter of fact. Either it will or it will not rain. We can use what evidence we have to figure out whether it will rain, but we will not know the truth, for certain, until tomorrow comes and goes. The day after tomorrow, we will know if it rained or not, so we will know the truth. To use another example, we may never know the truth about who assassinated President Kennedy. There does exist a truth about that question because he was assassinated, and a person or group of people did it, but we will likely never know, for certain, who did. There does exist a truth, because it is a matter of fact, not a matter of preference.

So critical thinking is a method we can use to try to arrive at the truth about something. Even if we never get to the absolute truth, we stand a better chance of getting close to the truth if we use critical thinking. We are more likely to find out if a car has mechanical problems if we examine the evidence than if we just go on our hunch. Critical thinking is a procedure we can use to get as close to the truth as possible, and it's more reliable than any other method.

Exercise 1.1

For each of the following situations, answer the following questions (A) Does a truth exist? Explain. (B) Will the people concerned perceive the truth differently? Why? (C) How might you determine the truth?

Situation #1

Richard and Liz are working in the same department. Richard is responsible for handling the petty cash account. When he went on vacation last week, he asked Liz to take over for him. He returned this week to find that over $200 was missing. Richard accused Liz of losing the money. Liz claims she handled everything correctly, and that it must have been missing before Richard left.

Situation #2

Bert and Ernie both work in the personnel department. Each has had considerable experience working with human resource development. Bert has been studying the idea of the entire office moving toward a four-day workweek. He believes that it has a number of distinct advantages, including improving morale, increasing productivity, and increasing the utilization of resources. Ernie disagrees. He is afraid that people will be less productive working longer days and that it will cost more money because of more human error brought on by fatigue.

Situation #3

George and Martha are both members of a team interviewing candidates for the position of receptionist/switchboard operator. Martha has decided that John would be the best candidate because he has excellent interpersonal skills. She would prefer to have someone who can relate well to people even if he does not have much clerical experience. She thinks the first impression outsiders get is crucial. George, on the other hand, knows that the person will be very busy and that managers will often give this person typing or other clerical work to do. He prefers to hire Jane who has secretarial experience, even though she is very shy and does not have much experience working with the public. "She'll learn," he claims. The question is who will do the best job?

Exercise 1.2

Find an article from the newspaper that has to do with the search for truth. It could be an article about a trial, about a scientific research study, or about some other topic involving the search for truth.

Title of Article:

Date:

Source Publication:

Identify the "truth" that is being sought in this situation:

What is the likelihood of finding the "absolute" truth in this case? Why?

Is the truth worth seeking in this case? Why?

Are individuals going to likely disagree about the existence of this truth? Why?

What specific actions might be taken to try to arrive closer to the truth? Explain:

Exercise 1.3

Think of a time, at home or at work, when it was important for you to find the truth.

Explain the situation.

Explain what methods you used to try to determine the truth.

Do you think you actually determined the truth?

What difficulties did you encounter getting to the truth?

CHAPTER 2
What It Means to Be a Critical Thinker

Critical thinkers regularly practice certain identifiable skills and behaviors. This chapter will discuss these characteristics of skilled thinkers:

> Practicing Constructive Skepticism
> Asking Useful Questions
> Listening Actively
> Practicing Fairmindedness
> Accepting Ignorance
> Flexibility
> Metacognition

Practicing Constructive Skepticism

Effective thinkers all share a characteristic skepticism. They are not willing to accept the conventional view without question. In a conversation, when a speaker brings up a point that is central to the argument, an alert thinker will not simply accept the idea without ample evidence. To a critical thinker, many statements are open to inquiry, even if the majority of people consider them to be true.

This is particularly valuable when the source of the statement is respected and assumed to be knowledgeable. Take the network news, for example. If a network anchorman reports the results of a scientific study linking decaffeinated coffee to heart disease, the average viewer will likely assume the evidence for such a connection is strong; otherwise it would not be reported. As most scientists would tell us, many studies suffer from significant research problems, which make their results questionable. In order to understand whether the results of a study are reliable, we would need to learn all the significant facts about the research methods, and even then we might reach a false conclusion. The network news programs may allot barely thirty seconds to such a story, hardly enough time to explain all the important information. We should always be skeptical of such information until we have reason to believe that we have enough information at our disposal to make an informed decision. This is rarely the case in a network news broadcast.

We should work at becoming more skeptical in all aspects of our lives. Many of us are already skeptical when listening to a sales pitch for a product or to a political speech. How skeptical are we when it comes to listening to a rumor at work? How likely are we to believe someone who thinks he knows what is wrong with our car, or who thinks she knows more about raising children than we do.

It is particularly important, and difficult, to practice skepticism when reading. Just because an author has researched a subject does not mean that everything he states is one hundred percent correct. For some reason, people tend to believe more of what they read than of what they hear. I remember overhearing two students discussing some controversial issue after class one day. One student, apparently practicing skepticism, asked where the first student got her information. "I read it," she replied. That ended the skeptical inquiry. The first student was willing to accept the point on face value simply because it had appeared in print! A skeptical student would have asked where she had read it, who wrote it, and what qualified that person to write it. As readers, we continually need to question what we are reading to see if it stands up to our inquiry.

Although we should practice being skeptical, we should keep it constructive. Questioning every small point in an argument is fruitless and may well antagonize the speaker and alienate others needlessly. It's important not to accept things on face value, but we have to choose our battles. Questioning trivial or well-accepted ideas is rarely going to be useful. This, however, is not the most common problem. The world is full of people who are more than willing to accept what they hear and read as fact.

Asking Useful Questions

Being able to ask pertinent, probing questions is, arguably, the single most important skill used by critical thinkers. It enables us to use all the other skills. Without being able to ask the right questions, we will miss opportunities to uncover false thinking and get to the truth. Unfortunately, most adults have not developed this skill and even consider it impolite to ask too many questions.

As we discussed earlier, children are natural critical thinkers. They ask questions continually. From the time toddlers wake up in the morning, if they are not exploring, they are asking questions, collecting information about this wonderful world we live in. It is through those questions that they learn. Yet as they mature, they learn that too many questions annoy people, so they stop asking. The result is an adult population too willing to accept what they hear.

As we work to become critical thinkers, we need to reawaken our need to ask questions. Even if we don't ask them out loud, we need to think questions to ourselves. For any provocative statement, we should be able to ask many questions. Consider the examples below:

From a network news report: "The president's new proposal for educational reform will most likely be met with stiff opposition in Congress."

What, exactly, is the president proposing?

What problem or problems is he trying to solve?

What aspect of education is he claiming to reform?

What evidence do we have that the reform is wise?

How did he arrive at the decision to propose these reforms?

How much will this reform cost?

What are the opinions of educational specialists?

Is he receiving pressure from special interest groups? If so, which ones?

What do his opponents claim is the problem with his proposal?

What, if anything, do they suggest as an alternative?

From a magazine article: "Health professionals suggest a diet low in saturated fat prevents heart disease."

Is this advice accepted by everyone?

To what health professionals is the article referring?

Why is a diet low in saturated fats likely to prevent heart disease?

How does saturated fat differ from other types of fat?

Are some types of fat okay to eat?

How much saturated fat is safe to eat?

What do those health professionals who disagree say? What do they suggest?

From a critical thinking teacher: "Critical Thinking is an important course which may help you in many areas of your life in the years ahead."

How do you know?

Why is it so important? Is it equally important to everyone?

How, specifically, will critical thinking instruction help me?

Are you suggesting it will help me later but not now? Why?

What evidence do you have to suggest that this course has helped your past students?

Are all critical thinking courses alike? If not, how did you decide what to include in this course? Why do you think this is the best way to organize such a course?

Obviously we can't ask every question that pops into our minds. The important thing is that we develop skeptical minds receptive to such questions. Even if we just ask the questions to ourselves, they will help clarify possible problems with a position we are considering. If the issue is important to us, we will most likely want to ask some questions. By not asking questions, we guarantee we will be making uninformed decisions.

Of course, asking good questions presupposes we will be prepared to listen to the answers actively.

Listening Actively

Listening is not the same as hearing. We can hear someone say something without actually listening to what that person is saying. Hearing consists of having the sound waves enter our ears and be perceived by the hearing center in the brain. It does not consist of focusing on the meaning of the sound or words. Listening is being able to decipher the meaning and significance of what we are hearing.

Think about your listening skills. How well do you listen when you are having a discussion? If you are like most people, when you are having a disagreement, you are spending most of your time thinking about what you are going to say next, and how you are going to respond to the speaker rather than listening to what the other person is saying. This generally leads nowhere because neither person is listening to what the other person is saying. The result is a lack of understanding on the part of both speakers, and the conflict cannot be resolved.

Listening well requires concentration. If we really want to understand someone's point, we have to focus on exactly what they are saying and make sure we understand before we respond. We cannot respond to a point we do not thoroughly understand! Yet, this is exactly what happens during most verbal disagreements. Let's look at the following example:

> John: Today you really made me mad when you criticized me in front of our friends.

> Connie: Well, you deserved it. I didn't want to get lost, but you were the one who insisted we didn't need to get directions from someone.

> John: You didn't even care that it was embarrassing me. I felt as though you were mocking me and it made me angry.

> Connie: This isn't the first time this has happened. Remember last Christmas when we got lost in New York? We wasted two hours, and we were late to my parents' house for Christmas dinner.

> John: If you hadn't been so negative, assuming I didn't know where I was going, I would probably have figured it out on my own. It gets me all worked up when you criticize me in front of other people. Why do you always do that?

Connie: Men! Why are they so stubborn? If it were me, I would have asked for directions.

Obviously, neither John nor Connie is doing much real listening. They are each talking at the other person without getting anywhere. It's easy to tell that this conversation is not going to end with a clear resolution.

Let's try this conversation again, and this time we will make Connie a good listener:

John: Today you really made me mad when you criticized me in front of our friends.

Connie: When I criticized you? Why did that make you mad?

John: I was embarrassed that you ridiculed me in front of everyone.

Connie: How did I do that?

John: When I didn't want to ask for directions, you started saying how I was a typical stubborn male who couldn't stand to ask for help.

Connie: Were you being stubborn?

John: Probably. Yes, but when you pointed that out, it made me feel angry, like I couldn't back down.

Connie: Back down?

John: Yes. By changing my mind and asking for directions it would make me look like I didn't know what I was doing.

In this dialogue, Connie is obviously listening to John. She may eventually respond to him, but not until she really understands what John is saying, why he is so upset. Chances are better they will reach some type of resolution if they practice good listening skills.

You may have noticed from this dialogue that one person was doing most of the listening. It is common to focus on one point of view at a time when practicing active listening. If both participants are active listeners, both will have a chance to explore each other's reasoning. You also may have noticed that questioning and listening are often used together. Questions can be a valuable resource for an active listener because they help clarify the speaker's ideas.

When we are discussing a difficult issue with someone, we can use a combination of questioning and listening to get an accurate idea of the person's ideas. In this type of dialogue, sometimes called **Socratic questioning**, the questioner must listen closely to what the speaker is saying and base his subsequent questions on what the speaker actually says. Consider this example:

Max: I don't think anyone should burn the American flag.

Susan: Why?

Max: Because it's the symbol for our country.

Susan: Are you saying it is wrong to destroy such a symbol?

Max: Yes.

Susan: Why?

Max: Because it seems wrong to me. We value the flag as a treasured symbol. It shows disrespect to burn it.

Susan: Disrespect in what sense?

Max: In the sense that people have died to defend that flag. It would be disrespectful to their memory to burn the flag.

Susan: Would it matter why the flag was burned?

Max: No, I don't think so.

Susan: So, burning the flag for any reason would be wrong?

Max: Except to dispose of it when it is worn out.

Susan: But burning the flag as a protest would be wrong?

Max: Absolutely.

Susan: Why?

Max: There are other ways to protest.

Susan: Some forms of protest are unacceptable?

Max: Yes. It's wrong if it offends people.

Susan: Wouldn't many kinds of protest offend some people?

Max: Yes, but burning the flag offends many people.

Susan: But not all people?

Max: No, not all. Some would not be offended, but most would.

Susan: Should we limit all protest to activities that don't offend people?

Max: Of course not. Protests will inevitably offend some people. That's the idea.

Susan: So, how is burning the flag different?

Max: I'm not sure. It seems to me there has to be some limit on protests.

Susan: Who would decide what the limits should be?

Max: I'm not sure, but it seems as though there should be some limit.

This dialogue is not finished, but it is getting somewhere. This is exactly what this type of questioning is designed to do: to reveal and explore someone's reasoning so we can better understand. It obviously requires that we listen actively. We cannot engage in Socratic questioning unless we pay close attention to what the person is saying and resist the temptation to argue.

Socratic questioning can be useful in a number of ways. It can be an excellent way to resolve conflict. By thoroughly understanding what someone is thinking, you can often find common ground and avoid senseless arguing. If you disagree with someone's point of view, try engaging him in Socratic questioning. Everyone likes to express his point of view, especially when someone is listening closely. If you learn to ask pointed, focused questions that closely follow his responses, you may reveal to him that his logic is weak. Or, you may convince yourself that his logic is better than you first thought. At the very least, you will assure that both of you understand his opinion more closely, which is essential if you are to resolve the conflict. It is not as confrontational as arguing, but it is usually more useful.

Socratic questioning takes practice. The most important thing to remember is to LISTEN carefully to what the person is saying and base your next question on exactly what the person says. Do not add your own ideas or argue, or you will be making the conversation your own, which is not helpful. Remember, your goal is to listen carefully and understand exactly what the other person is thinking.

Listed below are some suggested questions you might use to keep the conversation going in an appropriate way. (This information taken in modified form from Richard Paul's book, *Critical Thinking: What Every Person Needs to Know in a Rapidly Changing World*, Rohnert Park, CA: Center of Critical Thinking and Moral Critique, Sonoma State University 1990.) Try to become familiar with the questions so you can use them without referring to the list as you ask questions.

QUESTIONS OF CLARIFICATION

What do you mean by _____?
What is your main point?
Let me see if I understand. Do you mean_____?
Could you give me an example?
Why do you say this?

QUESTIONS THAT ASK FOR REASONS AND EVIDENCE

How do you know?
Why do you think this is true?
Why do you believe this?
What other information would we need to know this?
Why do you say that?
What led you to that belief?
How do you know about this?
Where did you get your information?

QUESTIONS ABOUT VIEWPOINTS OR PERSPECTIVES (GOOD TO USE WHEN YOU'RE STUCK)

What would someone who disagrees with you say?
Can you imagine why anyone might disagree with you?
     What might they say?
     How would you respond to them?
Can you think of alternatives to your position?

Remember, most of the questions you ask will be suggested directly by the response given. Try to follow up on the response to formulate your next question. Do not introduce new information. Your opinion DOES NOT MATTER. Your exclusive goal is to thoroughly understand the person's reasoning. If the reasoning is weak, it should become obvious.

To engage in effective Socratic questioning, you must always try to:

1. Listen carefully to exactly what your partner is saying.

2. Base each question on the previous answer as much as possible. This keeps you focused on what your partner is actually saying.

3. Resist the temptation to bring up your own ideas or debate with your partner. You can explore the ideas he brings up, but do not argue or add your own thoughts. Focus exclusively on what he is saying.

4. Practice! It is difficult to master Socratic questioning. It takes lots of practice. Don't get discouraged if you don't do well in the beginning.

Practicing Fairmindedness

There are at least two sides to every question. When we hold a particular point of view on a controversial question, we can be sure that other reasonable people will disagree. As critical thinkers, we must try to understand all points of view, even if they differ from our own. This makes sense for several reasons. First, unless we know what the opposing view is, how can we be certain we disagree with it? We cannot disagree with something we do not understand. Further, if we are to be in a position to argue for our point of view, we must be able to understand what the opponents will say, so we can respond to them. The arguer who understands the reasoning behind all points of view will be more effective.

We refer to the ability to seek out and understand alternative points of view as fairmindedness. Critical thinkers work to develop a healthy sense of fairmindedness. Let's look at an example:

Assume you are a taxpayer who is concerned with the high property taxes in your city. The school board has just proposed a bond issue to build a new elementary school. The estimates are that the average taxpayer will owe an additional seventy-five to one hundred dollars per year to finance this bond. You are opposed to this because you have watched taxes increase 145% since you moved into your home twelve years ago. You know of several cases in which elderly citizens have had to give up their homes because they could not afford to pay the taxes. The school department says they need a new school, but you know they are planning to close down one of the older buildings after they open the new school. It makes no sense to you to build a new school and tear an old one down. You are committed to your position to oppose the bond issue.

Before you vote, you owe it to yourself and to your community to practice fairmindedness. What is the argument being used to justify the new school? You call the chair of the school committee to find out. She claims that the district is projecting an increased enrollment over the next ten years and will need a bigger school to accommodate the children. When you ask about the school they are shutting down, she explains that they had a consultant conduct an investigation to determine the feasibility of refurbishing the old building. It was determined that the old building could be brought up to speed at a cost of about half of the cost of building a new school. However, it would accommodate only 230 children, whereas the new school is expected to accommodate about 700, enough to meet the district's needs. When you express your concern about taxes going up, she makes the point that although taxes would go up, the cost of not building the school could be higher. If the enrollment does increase as forecast, the district would be forced to add temporary classrooms, build a new building, or pay tuition to send the extra children to another community.

In her view, the most reasonable and cost effective solution to the problem is to bite the bullet and build the new school now.

So, does having the other view change your original position? Maybe. Maybe not, but at least you know both sides. Only by being aware of the arguments for and against the bond issue can you make an intelligent decision. If everyone in the community were as aware of both arguments, the best possible decision could be made. If each side is only aware of their own point of view, then the decision will be political instead of rational. All too often, this is the case.

So, practice fairmindedness. Examine your beliefs and positions from time to time and try to figure out what those who oppose your view might argue. You may need to do research. You may need to ask your opponents. The results may surprise you.

Accepting Ignorance

What does it mean to be ignorant? Is it a bad thing to be ignorant? Are smart people ignorant? What can I do about my ignorance?

All humans are ignorant about most things. Ignorance means not knowing. As we have already discussed in the last chapter, it is often very difficult to know the truth about something, particularly if we do not have access to all the information we need. As a result, there are many issues we know little or nothing about. As a critical thinker, we should value our ignorance. VALUE OUR IGNORANCE? Yes, because it is important for a critical thinker to understand the depths of his ignorance before he can understand what he needs to do to overcome it. In this way, our ignorance becomes an asset to a critical thinker. If he knows he doesn't know something, he can find out. If he doesn't know he doesn't know, he's in trouble.

To uncritical thinkers, knowing little or nothing about a topic does not stop them from having opinions. We all know many people who have views about things they know little about. Of course, they're entitled to their opinions, but we are entitled to recognize their opinions as uninformed and worthless. They do not believe their opinions are uninformed because they have no sense of the degree of their ignorance.

Why are we all so ignorant? To put it simply, it's because there is so much to know about the world, even the most knowledge-hungry people can know only a small fraction of what there is to know. Albert Einstein was ignorant about many things. He certainly was not ignorant about physics, but he was most likely very ignorant about neurosurgery, Louisiana Cajun music, and Irish mythology. Obviously, no one can know all there is to know.

For some people, the most difficult three words to speak are, "I don't know." Many uncritical thinkers hate to admit they don't know about something, so they construct the reality about that subject from the little information they do have. They often

HALF PRICE BOOKS ®

Half Price Books
3860 LA REUNION PKWY
DALLAS, TX 75212
OFS OrderID 4024520

Thank you for your order, Alicia Neal!

Thank you for shopping with Half Price Books! Please contact service15@hpb.com. if you
have any questions, comments or concerns about your order (104-2947574-4588259)

SKU	ISBN/UPC	Title & Author/Artist	Shelf ID	Qty
U169209268	9780757520013	FIGURING THINGS OUT: A PRACTICAL GUII REF 18.3 FRAYER WILLIAM		1

SHIPPED STANDARD TO:
Alicia Neal
1947 CONKLE RD
RIVERDALE GA 30296-2822

ORDER# **104-2947574-4588259**
AmazonMarketplaceUS

convince themselves they know considerably more than they do. This can lead to thinking errors and poor decisions. There is no shame in recognizing we do not know something; in fact, it is necessary before we can start to correct the situation. A critical thinker tries to be aware of the areas she knows little about. When someone asks her what her position about the proposed bond issue is, she might respond by saying, "I really don't know that much about it. I'll have to read more about the proposal before I can form an opinion." Pretending or assuming we know all there is to know on a subject can be a serious mistake.

Students frequently make this mistake when they start searching for a job after graduating from college. They have some preconceived ideas about the types of jobs that are available and the positions for which they are qualified. So they start applying, assuming they know exactly what they want to do. Too often, they neglect to find some exciting opportunities only because they were ignorant of them. Had they known enough to accept their ignorance and do some research to find out, they may have been surprised to find some additional job opportunities. In this way, accepting our ignorance can help us understand what information we still need to make better decisions.

To be ignorant is to be human. Value your ignorance because it provides an opportunity to learn.

Flexibility

The other three most difficult words to speak are, "I was wrong." Admitting error is at least as difficult as admitting ignorance because it implies that we are fallible. Of course we are, but we don't like to think about it because it can damage our view of ourselves.

Being able to change our minds is being able to admit we were wrong, and there's no crime in being wrong. In fact, there are many legitimate reasons for being wrong: we might not have had all the information, we might have been working with incorrect information, we might have been making incorrect assumptions, or we might simply have made an error in reasoning. The problem, as with ignorance, is not being wrong, but being wrong and not knowing it.

People who have difficulty admitting error often place themselves in the awkward position of maintaining the correctness of their position while everyone around them knows they are wrong. When faced with considerable evidence that she is wrong, a critical thinker will reconsider her position to account for the new evidence. When an uncritical thinker is faced with the same situation, she will most likely dig in her heels and try to justify her position in the face of the contrary evidence. The critical thinker, after changing her mind can move on to do what is necessary, not worrying about whether she was right or wrong. The uncritical thinker will remain stuck, protecting her unreasonable position to avoid having to change her mind.

History is full of examples when tragedies occurred or were compounded by the failure of world leaders to change their minds in the face of overwhelming evidence that it would have been prudent to do so. President Lyndon Johnson stubbornly refused to pull out of Vietnam even after it was clear our involvement was doing no good. The leaders of the former Soviet Union stood tenaciously by their cooperative, government-run farm system in spite of its obvious inefficiency and corruption. The South African government maintained their apartheid system of segregation for many years even though the benefits of eliminating racial discrimination were obvious to many white leaders.

The best reason for changing our minds is that it works better than not changing our minds. We can count on being incorrect a certain percentage of the time. We will make poor decisions. We will make incorrect assumptions. We will be wrong about many things. Failing to admit our failure will just delay the inevitable and may often complicate the situation by leading to other problems. We gain nothing by standing by a position we know is indefensible. Good thinkers realize this.

Metacognition

Because thinking is a set of skills, we can improve our thinking by practicing. The problem is, most of us are not aware of the skills we are using. How can we practice a skill we are not conscious of? Good thinkers have developed the habit of thinking about their own thinking. This ability is called metacognition. It is important that we recognize the strengths and weaknesses of our thinking and work to improve our thinking skills. Let's look at a few examples:

You are in the market for a newer vehicle. Since you are like most students, and have very limited funds, you decide you can only afford 1,000 dollars for a vehicle that you hope will last the next year and a half until you graduate from college. You visit a few used car lots and find nothing good in your price range. At the next car lot you find a bright red Ford Mustang with high mileage and a sticker price of 1,250 dollars. You ask to drive it and it seems to be in decent shape. You have an overwhelming desire to buy the car, but you only want to spend 1,000 dollars. You ask the salesperson if he will take 1,000 dollars, and he agrees. You are on the verge of purchasing the car.

STOP! Now is the time to use critical thinking. If you think about your thinking, you may realize that you are letting your excitement overtake you. You can imagine driving the car home and showing your friends. You are aware of this and you know that you are not thinking logically. Because you are aware of it, you tell the salesperson that you need some time to think about it. You are giving yourself the time to use some critical thinking. You realize you should call the previous owner, have it checked out by a mechanic, and get more information about that particular model and year from the library. If you had not been aware of your thinking, and the fact that you tend to act impulsively when making major purchases, you might not have taken the time to actually apply your critical thinking skills. This is why metacognition helps; it enables you to see what's going on so you can make better choices.

Consider another example:

It is mid-October in a presidential election year. You are facing choices for president, senator, representative, several state and local offices and two referendum initiatives. You have not been paying much attention to the election because you are not particularly interested in politics. Nevertheless, you do vote because you believe in democracy and consider it your duty to exercise your opportunity to vote. For the last several elections, you have not made up your mind for whom to vote until you were actually in the voting booth, and you ended up casting some votes without knowing much about the candidates or the issues. You felt badly about those votes because you were not confident you were making good choices. This time, you are determined to avoid the same problem, yet you already see the same thing is happening again.

STOP! Think about your thinking. Consider what's happening. You realize the problem is with your thinking. You are not comfortable with the complex reasoning required to make an intelligent decision. You have no problem thinking through a complicated problem at work or for a home construction problem, but you have no appetite for politics, so you are not interested in spending a long time thinking about it. So, as you think about your thinking, you realize that the problem is one of time and energy. Using critical thinking, you can now develop a strategy for becoming informed enough to make a good decision. You may decide to pay more attention to particular races because they are more important to you. You may seek out articles in the newspaper, which compare the stands of the candidates. You may watch a few public affairs programs, which analyze the candidates' stands on the issues. You are practicing metacognition by being aware of the fact that you were not examining the choices thoughtfully because you were uncomfortable with the complexity of the problem. Only by becoming aware of your thinking process can you improve it.

Good thinkers can take a step back from a situation and examine their own thinking process. They can recognize their biases, identify any thinking errors, and work to correct them. Uncritical thinkers are unaware of their thinking process. How can they improve a process if they are not aware of it?

Exercise 2.1

Consider each of the following sources. Explain why you would or would not tend to believe each source. Then, see if you can create derive a general rule about when to be skeptical. The first example is completed for you.

a. A story about aliens in the *National Enquirer.*

<u>Would you believe it? Why?</u> *No. This publication is not known for being a reliable source of news. Its goal is entertainment. Most readers do not take it seriously.*

<u>General rule:</u> *Be skeptical when the source is known to be unreliable.*

b. A story about aliens in the *New York Times.*

<u>Would you believe it? Why?</u>

<u>General rule:</u>

c. A study on the effect of fat in the diet conducted by the American Heart Association.

<u>Would you believe it? Why?</u>

<u>General rule:</u>

d. A lecture from your math instructor on how to solve quadratic equations.

<u>Would you believe it? Why?</u>

<u>General rule:</u>

e. Information about a car from a used car salesperson.

Would you believe it? Why?

General rule:

f. Dietary benefits of oatmeal as outlined on the following website: www.quakeroats.com

Would you believe it? Why?

General rule:

g. Information about a company for which you're interested in working for from a friend of yours who already works there.

Would you believe it? Why?

General rule:

h. A job reference provided by the applicant's sister.

Would you believe it? Why?

General rule:

Exercise 2.2

By the time you do this assignment, you will have been assigned a controversial topic in class. Using this topic, complete the following worksheet:

Topic:

How much do you know about the topic? Is this a topic with which you are very familiar? Which aspects of the topic are you most informed or most ignorant about?

What do you, personally, consider the most reasonable position on this issue?

List as many reasons as you can to support your position. Try to make each reason a complete sentence:

1.

2.

3.

4.

5.

6.

7.

8.

9.

10.

Practice fairmindedness by listing any reasons you can think of OPPOSING your position:

1.

2.

3.

4.

5.

6.

7.

8.

9.

10.

Exercise 2.3

Carefully read the article handed out with this assignment. After you're finished, generate as many questions as you can about the article and the information in the article. Narrow your questions down to the ten most substantive questions. For the assignment, (A) list each question, and (B) explain why having the answer to that question will help you to understand the article or the issue better.

Exercise 2.4

Practice Socratic questioning with at least two people. You might ask them to help you with this assignment and try to learn their views on some relevant issue. Or, you might find a good opportunity to use this technique in your work, at home with your family, or even in school. Once you've tried it at least twice, answer the following questions:

  a. Did you find that trying Socratic questioning was different than having a normal conversation? Explain how.

  b. What was the most difficult thing about using Socratic questioning?

  c.. Can you think of any circumstances in your life when using Socratic questioning might be useful? Explain.

Exercise 2.5

Considering the work we have done in the class so far, consider how good a thinker you are. Write two paragraphs, (A) one in which you discuss a recent example when you used critical thinking, and (B) one in which you failed to use critical thinking. Please use examples that you would not mind sharing with the class.

CHAPTER 3
Avoiding the Pitfalls of Weak Thinking

So far, we have discussed the characteristics of good thinking. It is also important, of course, to avoid weak, or faulty, thinking. Thinking errors, sometimes called fallacies, are commonly encountered and can easily fool the unwary thinker.

This chapter introduces thirteen of the most common thinking errors. Some of these errors are committed inadvertently. Others are used consciously to persuade when logic, alone, is not sufficient. For the purpose of our discussion, these errors are divided into the following four categories:

- Errors based on insufficient evidence
- Errors based on oversimplification
- Errors based on emotion
- Errors based on evasion

As you read about each of these errors, think of examples, either from your own thinking or from arguments you've encountered from television or other sources. Try to understand the essential weakness of each error and learn to detect it when you encounter it in the future. Being able to label an error helps you remember to notice it when you see it.

Errors Based on Insufficient Evidence

The process of reasoning consists of gathering evidence in order to formulate a reasonable conclusion. It is important to have enough good evidence to draw a sound conclusion. Not having enough evidence, or using faulty evidence, can cause us to draw an incorrect conclusion. The three errors that relate to a lack of evidence include the following:

- Jumping to conclusions
- Stereotyping
- Circular reasoning (begging the question)

Jumping to Conclusions

The most basic error based on insufficient evidence is prematurely jumping to a conclusion.

As we have already discussed, critical thinking is most useful when it helps us make decisions. When we reason carefully, we collect evidence, and when we are sure we have enough, we arrive at a conclusion. Hopefully, our conclusion is accurate because it is based on reliable information. Even if we have not arrived at the absolute truth, we have increased the probability that we have made an informed decision.

This process is not quick. One of the problems with critical thinking is that it often takes a considerable amount of time to gather enough information to reach the most reasonable decision. Often we may feel we do not have enough time to go through this process. We can be tempted to take shortcuts. This usually takes the form of drawing a hasty or premature conclusion based on insufficient evidence.

This error can occur even among the best thinkers. How do we know when we have enough evidence to draw a reasonable conclusion? We may think we have enough facts, so we draw a conclusion. When more facts become evident, it throws our conclusion into question. This frequently happens in science. Aristotle reached the conclusion that the sun, moon, planets and the stars all rotated around the earth which, he believed, was at the center of the universe. This was reasonable at the time, based on the evidence available to him. In fact, his ideas held up for over one thousand years. Centuries later, however, Copernicus used more up-to-date evidence to draw a different conclusion: the earth actually revolved around the sun. As it turned out, Aristotle's conclusions were based on insufficient evidence.

The practice of medicine has also been fraught with premature conclusions. Previously, patients recovering from major surgery were kept resting in bed for several weeks while their wounds healed. Today, as any surgical patient knows, the nursing staff will insist that the patient get out of bed almost immediately. This new thinking was based on clinical evidence that suggested that patients who remained immobile suffered more postsurgical complications than those who were exercised shortly after surgery.

A more contemporary example involves the media's rush to judgment when an airliner crashes. Matthew Wald, in an article for the *New York Times* (November 6, 1999) reported that the initial theory about why airliners crash, the one often reported by the media, is very often incorrect. He points out that crash investigations are complex and take a great deal of time. But in our search to find answers, we tend to jump to premature conclusions. He cites many examples of erroneous initial conclusions. Typical is the example of an Indonesian crash of a Boeing 737 in 1997. When investigators first found the wreckage, it appeared that the rivets holding the engine on had come loose, a manufacturing error. But after a thorough investigation, it was determined that the rivets had loosened as a *result* of the accident, and were not the cause of the accident.

Many have claimed that the decision to go to war with Iraq in 2003 was based on insufficient evidence. In justifying his case for war, President George W. Bush and members of his administration argued that our intelligence sources indicated that Saddam Hussein, the president of Iraq, had massive amounts of weapons of mass destruction (WMD's) which were posing a direct threat to U.S. security. As we now know, very little evidence of these weapons was uncovered after the war. This is a good example of jumping to a conclusion.

In all of these cases, the conclusions seemed reasonable at the time but later proved to be based on insufficient evidence. We need to draw conclusions and make decisions based on the evidence we have available at the moment. It is very easy to assume we have enough evidence and draw a conclusion that seems justifiable at the moment but can prove to be wrong. Consider these scenarios:

> You are the parent of a teenage daughter who has an 11:30 p.m. curfew. She is usually reliable about being home on time. It is now 1 a.m. She is not home, and you have not received a phone call. Do you conclude she has been in an accident? Do you conclude that she's up to no good? As tempting as it may be, you do not have enough information on which to base either of those conclusions at this point. There are several realistic alternative conclusions to consider, including that she had car trouble and is unable to get to a phone.

> You are a high school math teacher. Tony and Sam sit next to each other. Sam is an excellent student. His test average is 98.5%. Tony has failed every exam this semester. Today they both handed in a test. You graded it, and Tony received a 100, just like Sam. Do you conclude that Tony cheated? Perhaps, but it is possible that Tony studied and earned his higher grade. It is tempting to reach a premature conclusion.

> You have been dating your boyfriend, Jacques, for the past year and a half. You are very serious and plan to marry. Today, your best friend, Susan, tells you that she saw Jacques in a restaurant last night having dinner with a very pretty young woman. Jacques told you he was going to stay home and study last night. What do you conclude? Would you be justified in concluding that Jacques is dating another woman? What alternative conclusions could be reached? As a critical thinker, you should talk to Jacques before reaching any conclusion.

These are all situations in which you might be tempted to jump to an incorrect conclusion. It is one of the most common thinking errors. As a good thinker, be careful before reaching any conclusion. When you are considering a possible conclusion, ask yourself several questions:

> Do I have enough information to reach this conclusion?

> Where could I get more information?

> Are there alternative conclusions I might reach that would fit with the evidence I have?

If you decide you simply don't have enough information, avoid making a conclusion at all. If you think you have enough information, but you are not certain, make your conclusion tentative. Qualify your conclusion by saying, "Based on what I know..." or, "If the information I have now is correct..." This will allow you room to change your mind later if more plausible evidence becomes available.

Finally, remember that conclusions that may seem reasonable today can be very wrong tomorrow. When you make conclusions, be sure you have examined all the evidence that is available because you could be incorrect. If you don't have enough information, don't arrive at a conclusion. Admit you don't know.

Stereotyping

Stereotyping is another type of error that occurs when we try to draw a conclusion based on an insufficient amount of evidence.

To many people, stereotyping refers to a bias or prejudice against specific ethnic groups. We are all familiar with ethnic slurs or jokes that are based on stereotyping. This serious thinking error can apply to many other situations or groups as well. As we try to make sense of the world, we often use stereotyping, usually without realizing it.

Simply defined, stereotyping is an UNREASONABLE generalization. To generalize means to apply the characteristics of a few to a larger group. This is often appropriate. For example, when pollsters take opinion surveys, they question a small sample and generalize the results to the population as a whole. Another example of generalizing is when a lab technician takes only a sample of your blood and reasonably presumes that all your blood is essentially the same. These are examples of reasonable generalizations.

Stereotyping occurs when we generalize in an unreasonable way. In an opinion survey, a scientifically selected random sample assures that the results are likely to match the population as a whole, within a few percentage points. For this reason, we can consider this a reasonable generalization.

An unreasonable generalization is usually the result of an insufficient sample. A poor thinker may conclude that all Arabs are terrorists because some terrorists captured have an Arabic ethnic background. Popular stereotypes include lazy welfare recipients, rich Republicans, racist southerners, and effeminate gay men. These are stereotypes because although some members of these groups have these characteristics, many do not. These generalizations are unreasonable and not accurate.

When we extend this type of thinking to our nation, our church, or our ethnic group, we are often guilty of ethnocentric thinking. We see examples of this type of thinking all around us. Racism is a type of ethnocentric thinking when one believes his or her race to be superior to all others. We see religious wars fought over ethnocentrism in Northern Ireland and the Middle East. We have seen tribal warfare in many African nations. In many countries, including our own, we see a rise in ethnocentrism when we go to war. In every major war, the enemy is demonized to an unreasonable degree. The stereotypes of German and Japanese soldiers during World War II were reflected in war posters of that era. German and Japanese posters demonized the American and British forces. Today, the Israelis demonize the Palestinians as the Palestinians demonize the Israelis. Such ethnocentrism may be defended because it encourages patriotism and support for the war effort, but it does not encourage rational thinking.

Stereotyping is not limited to ethnocentric thinking or racism. We can stereotype by gender. For example, thinking that women cannot safely and efficiently perform work traditionally performed by men is a gender stereotype. Similarly, presuming that men are insensitive and unable to nurture small children is an equally unreasonable generalization. It may be true some of the time, but it is not reliably true.

Stereotyping can also include occupations (used car salespeople and hairdressers), home state (Texans and Californians), and even hair color (blonde jokes). We are familiar with stereotypes. The danger, however, is in believing they are true. We can understand the stereotype of Boston drivers being aggressive and rude, without really believing all Boston drivers are cut from the same mold. Understanding our culture (or any culture) requires that we understand the common stereotypes, but good thinkers recognize that all stereotypes are based on an insufficient amount of evidence and are, therefore, largely false.

Circular Reasoning (Begging the Question)

This error occurs when someone uses the conclusion itself as evidence to prove the conclusion true. This can also be referred to as "begging the question."

A popular example of this fallacy would be arguing that the Bible is the word of God because the Bible claims this to be true. No evidence is offered in this argument. The only reason offered is, essentially, the conclusion itself. If I agree that the Bible's claim about its infallibility is true, I have already accepted the conclusion. Therefore, this is a circular argument. In a standard argument, the arguer tries to get the reader or listener to accept a conclusion by providing reasons to support that conclusion.

Let's look at the following example for the death penalty:

> The death penalty is justified for three reasons. First, when
> someone murders another person, the punishment must be severe
> to deter future crimes. Second, society should not be forced to
> pay for a murderer's upkeep for the rest of his life, so the death

penalty makes economic sense. And finally, the death penalty is morally warranted in the case of premeditated murder, because this is a capital offense.

The first two reasons are reasonable: they provide statements which provide support for the conclusion. But the third reason actually restates the conclusion that the death penalty is justifiable. If we agree that premeditated murder is a capital offense, we have essentially agreed that we support capital punishment.

Let's consider another example. Consider the following argument:

When it comes to automobiles, you're better off buying a new vehicle. First, new vehicles come with a warranty to cover repairs for the first few years, which assures you of minimal maintenance costs. Second, new vehicles are worth more when you trade them in, so you can afford a better vehicle when you do trade. Finally, as we all know, you're better off buying anything new; it just makes sense.

In this argument, the third reason is begging the question. If we accept that reason, that we're always better off buying new, we've essentially accepted the conclusion itself.

We sometimes see this kind of error in political ads. For example, if an ad claims that the viewers should vote for Susan Jones because she "deserves our vote," this is begging the question. WHY does she deserve our vote? No evidence is given. If we accept the premise that she deserves our vote, we have essentially accepted the conclusion itself.

Errors Based on Oversimplification

The journalist H. L. Mencken once noted that "For every complex question there is a simple answer, and it is wrong." Most of the world's problems are indeed complex. As critical thinkers, we must be willing to engage ourselves in the complexity of a problem to find a reasonable answer. Many people avoid dealing with complicated problems because they find the process too troublesome.

It is easier to oversimplify a problem than to examine it in detail. In our attempt to understand the world, we try to see easy-to-understand patterns and solutions. Sometimes this leads us to good answers, but often it does not. Oversimplification can lead to one of the following errors:

· Blindly Accepting the Popular View

- Black and White Thinking
- The False Cause Fallacy
- Appeal to Authority
- False Analogy

Blindly Accepting the Popular View

Because we live in a democracy, we are used to the concept that the majority rules. It seems to be the fairest way to resolve conflicts. Take a vote and see who gets the most votes. This may be a good way to run a government, but it is not always a good way to determine which ideas are best. It is an oversimplification to presume that if more people believe something, then it must be true.

Unpopular ideas can often be the ones with the most merit. During the late 1930's, most British were in favor of staying out of World War II. They believed Hitler was not a serious threat to their national security. How wrong this view turned out to be when, in 1940, the Germans began their invasion in the Battle of Britain.

In 1980, in this country, Ronald Reagan was elected president and promised to try a new economic theory called supply side economics. Under this plan, taxes were cut drastically, especially for the wealthy, with the hope that it would induce economic prosperity that would "trickle down" to the middle class. His plan was enormously popular and sailed through both houses of Congress. Although Reaganomics infused much cash into the economy, many economists recognize the policy as a failure that quadrupled the deficit during Reagan's eight years in office. Even though Reagan's popularity persists after his death, and a popular view is that he was a good president, the truth about his economic policies remains the same.

Frequently, a view held by the majority of people is not based on solid evidence. This is particularly true in this age of mass media. When a particular view is reported prominently by the television networks, it increases the chances that more people will tend to agree with that view. Under these circumstances, it is more difficult for the average television viewer to get a balanced view of the issue because the opposing view is not reported as widely. So it becomes easier to go along with the commonly accepted view.

For example, it was a widespread belief that during the rollover from the year 1999 to 2000, the world, particularly less-developed countries, would experience potentially serious problems as a result of the Y2K computer problems. The news media trumpeted these problems, creating a sense of near-hysteria by New Year's Eve 1999. In reality, the problems across the globe were very minor.

Avoiding this kind of conformity is also important in our everyday lives. We all want to be liked and respected by our peers, but we need to avoid going along with the majority view when we have reason to believe it is wrong. Adolescents are, as we know, very susceptible to peer pressure. They will behave in ways that go against their better judgment in order to be accepted by the group. But how often, as adults, do we fall prey to the same type of pressures? Consider these examples:

> Somebody at a party tells a joke that you find insulting to a particular minority group. Do you go along with the joke and laugh, even if it goes against your personal belief systems? Is this harmful?

> Your boss at work has instituted a new work policy to eliminate waste. You haven't had time to think about it and consider its benefits, but your co-workers are ridiculing it as unnecessary. They ask you what you think. Do you go along or do you tell them you need more time to consider it?

> You are at a meeting. A person everyone respects has made a suggestion that seems like a bad idea to you. Immediately everyone joins in to support the idea because they like and respect the person who made the suggestion. Do you disagree openly?

In each of these situations, it may be tempting to conform to the majority view. To disagree openly with the group takes a certain amount of **intellectual courage**. A good thinker will consider disagreeing when she suspects the view of the majority may be incorrect. It is not easy to be an independent thinker, especially when there is considerable pressure to conform. Good thinkers base their decisions on evidence rather than on what is popular. So, as a critical thinker, you need to be ready to take an independent position if you are convinced it is correct.

Black and White Thinking

This error is another type of oversimplification. It occurs when an arguer suggests there are only two alternatives when, in fact, there could be others as well. Consider this statement, for example:

"You have a choice to make. You can either go to college, and make a success out of your life, or be doomed to a life of misery in a dead-end job." Although we would certainly agree that going to college increases your chance of landing a good job, it is a gross oversimplification to suggest that it's really as simple as the speaker suggests. In fact, some people are quite successful without attending college, while some college graduates find their jobs unfulfilling and miserable.

Our political leaders have a particular affinity for black and white thinking. This type of logic appeals to voters because it presents what seems to be be a simple solution, often appealing to common sense. It fails because it presents an overly simplistic view of reality. Consider the issue of gun control.

We obviously have a problem with gun-related crimes in this country. People are being killed with guns in the United States at an alarming rate, far more than in other industrialized countries. Some people see the solution to this problem in gun control; others believe gun control would not help and may, in fact, make the problem worse. Both sides of the gun control debate have a tendency to make this complex problem sound more black and white.

Those in favor of gun control believe the problem is having too many guns on the street. They reason that if fewer guns were sold, the problem would diminish. Those who oppose gun control assert that gun ownership is a right that is guaranteed by the Constitution and that if we limit gun ownership, only the criminals will have guns, making the problem worse.

Both sides treat the problem as a black and white issue. In reality, it is not that simple. Let's examine the complexity of the issue. Certainly the easy availability of firearms does put more guns into circulation, putting some in the hands of criminals. However, to suggest that simply reducing the number of guns people can own will reduce the gun-related crimes is probably not correct. Most criminals, as gun owners suggest, do not purchase their guns legally, which minimizes the effect of gun registration laws. On the other hand, the proliferation of guns in our society is a problem and we probably need to find a way to control this problem. If it is too easy to obtain a gun, some criminals will be able to obtain a gun easily to commit a particular crime. However, what about the roots of crime? Why do some people become sociopathic and shoot innocent people? Why is there such gang violence in our cities? Why do young children bring guns to schools in increasing numbers? The problem with violent behavior can be traced to many sources, including poverty, child abuse, alcohol and drug abuse, the mass media, and other sociological factors. To presume that gun control, or lack of gun control, alone, will have a significant effect on this trend is naive and a gross oversimplification. We need to examine the complex interrelation of various factors before we can hope to deal with this problem.

To use another political example, President George W. Bush, in declaring his war on terrorism after the September 11 attacks, declared to all other countries of the world: "You're either with us or you're with the terrorists." Although this declaration had wide appeal, it was a classic black and white oversimplification. Many of our European allies supported our goals in addressing Islamic fundamentalist terrorism, but they did not always agree with our methods, especially our preemptive attack on Iraq. Did that mean they were "with the terrorists"? Despite this black and white claim, our relations with other countries remain complex and rife with shades of gray. Black and white logic may appeal to voters in the short term, but it is intellectually dishonest and not terribly helpful in understanding a complex world.

False Cause (Post Hoc, Ergo Propter Hoc)

The false cause fallacy (sometimes referred to by its Latin name: post hoc, ergo propter hoc) is one of the most prevalent. It occurs when we presume that because one event PRECEDED a second event, it actually CAUSED that event.

Let's look at another historical example. In 1992, George H. W. Bush was running for reelection against Bill Clinton and H. Ross Perot. The economy had weakened after the 1990 Gulf War. Bill Clinton used the argument that because Bush was president when the economy weakened, he must have caused this economic downturn. In reality, as many economists suggest, economic recessions are natural economic cycles influenced by many factors, and the policies of a particular president may not have a strong impact on the relative strength or weakness of the economy. Nevertheless, Clinton's point stuck, and voters blamed President Bush for the faltering economy, electing Bill Clinton. Similarly, when the economy showed strength in 1996, Clinton was easily reelected as voters connected his policies with a strong economy. In these examples, many voters (and the media) may actually be guilty of committing a false cause error.

Many superstitious beliefs are the result of false cause thinking. Imagine a professional baseball player mired in a bad hitting slump, not having had a hit for ten games. If, one day, that player forgets to shave then proceeds to get three hits in that day's game, it might be likely that the player would presume that the failure to shave CAUSED him to get those hits. It is unlikely he would shave anytime soon! Although the presence of extra facial hair did not likely cause those extra hits, the confidence inspired by his coincidental success might help his batting average. This is a typical example of a post hoc fallacy.

A variation of this false cause fallacy is the belief that if two events are correlated (tend to occur together), that one event caused the other event. We see this error occurring in many contexts. One common one involves scientific studies. Let's say researchers discover that people who drink five or more cups of coffee every day have a higher rate of heart disease than those who drink less coffee or no coffee. They may presume that drinking that much coffee CAUSES heart disease. In fact we do not know this. Just because excessive coffee drinking CORRELATES with heart disease does not mean it CAUSES heart disease. Perhaps, for example, those who drank more coffee also smoked, ate poorly, or failed to get enough exercise? How would we know which of these variables caused the heart disease? Remember: CORRELATION DOES NOT INDICATE CAUSATION.

The false cause error is very common. We can all think of examples when we may have fallen for this erroneous thinking. It is, of course, yet another oversimplification error. We ascribe causation to one event when the truth is more complex. There are often many variables which cause an event, not just one. Heart disease is caused by many factors, even if it happens to correlate with coffee drinking.

Appeal to Authority

This fallacy occurs when we suggest that we should accept the view of an expert or other authority without question. We are bombarded in the media by so-called "experts" who claim to explain world events, how to raise healthy children, and why all classrooms should be equipped with computers. Of course, we DO need experts, people who have studied these issues and have formulated thoughtful, informed opinions. The fallacy is in accepting someone's opinion, without question, simply because they claim to be an authority. No one's opinion should be accepted without question. To do so requires that we suspend our own reasoning.

Let's look at some examples. One situation when we tend to rely on authority is when seeking medical care. Of course, it is reasonable to rely on opinions of physicians and other medical professionals who are often prepared with years of study and clinical practice. It is unreasonable, however, to rely on the opinion of any one expert and treat the opinion as infallible. Most medical professionals understand that even the best clinicians can be wrong, and encourage second, even third opinions about important decisions. As critical thinkers, we should obviously rely on medical experts but not suspend our own thinking in the process. It's easier to rely completely on a physician, but being actively involved in your own care is more reasonable. It also increases the likelihood you'll have a better outcome.

We often encounter this in written arguments. Arguers will often back up their assertions with the testimony or opinions of experts. These opinions may or may not be valid. As readers, we need to know how qualified these experts are. We should try to learn if they have a biased view. In other words, do they have a preconceived view because of an emotional or financial connection to the issue? We should also try to determine whether these so-called experts agree with one another. Evaluating the opinions of knowledgeable sources is a complex, but necessary, process. Simply accepting the opinion of a physician, an auto mechanic, or even your critical thinking instructor, without question, is an oversimplification.

False Analogy

An analogy is a comparison between two concepts or ideas, usually for the purpose of clarification. It is often used to explain complex ideas. For example, when students start to learn about electricity, the instructor will frequently use the analogy of a garden hose. The water in the hose might be compared to the current in an electrical wire. The water pressure is comparable to the voltage. When we put a kink in the hose, this is similar to putting resistance in the wire. As the kink increases the water pressure and reduces the water flow, so does resistance increase voltage and reduce current. Although water hoses and electrical wires are, in most ways, very different, the analogy works because it helps us to understand the dynamics of current, resistance, and voltage.

Let's consider a couple of other brief examples. Government corruption might be compared to a cancer. It may start out as a small spot but could grow to cause serious problems unless it is removed in its early stages. We might also compare a college education to an insurance policy. Like insurance, an education provides a "safety net" for us. When economic conditions or personal circumstances take a downward turn, someone with a college degree will have a better chance of weathering the storm.

Analogies are, of course, limited. They are also a type of simplification. When we compare unlike things, it is often a simplification to suggest that they are alike in some ways when not alike in other important ways. Sometimes arguers use analogies to make a point in a faulty way. If the comparison is not a reasonable one, the analogy fails. Let's consider a few examples.

Raising children might be compared to tending a garden. The analogy actually works to a degree. To make a flower grow, we must provide a bed of fertile soil, lots of sunshine and water. Children need a safe environment, lots of love and nourishing food. Just as you can't make a flower grow by pulling on it, you can't rush child development. Children must grow at their own pace. But, of course, raising children is significantly more complex than tending a garden. If a flower is damaged, you can discard it. Children must be tended regardless of any damage they may suffer. They must be prepared for life, and taught the lessons they will need to live independently. You could never expect plants to live outside the garden! The flower analogy only goes so far. Ultimately, the analogy is too simple to be of any real use.

Another false analogy might be to compare one addiction to another. For example, we might compare tobacco addiction to overeating. An editorial writer might suggest, for example, that we should tax junk food the way we tax tobacco. After all, she might argue, both tobacco and junk food are addictive and potentially lethal. Nevertheless, the analogy is a weak one. The solution for tobacco addiction is to stop tobacco completely. Tobacco use has no redeeming values. Furthermore, the use of tobacco causes direct harm to others. Eating is a natural human process necessary for survival. People may make unwise choices about what and how much to eat, but they must eat something. And overeating has no harmful effects on others. So, as a public health problem, tobacco use and overeating are very different problems. Comparing them is an unhelpful oversimplification.

The terrorist attacks on the United States on September 11, 2001 have often been compared to the Japanese attack on Pearl Harbor in 1941. Some have argued that the surprise attacks are similar because they both caused massive loss of life and both led to wars. But the similarity between these two events is very limited. Pearl Harbor was an attack on one nation by another. The enemy was clearly identifiable, and Congress was able to declare war. Although the terrorist attacks led to the so-called "War on Terror," it is a much different kind of "war." The enemy is not clearly defined, which has led to some confusion and difficulty in knowing how to wage battle. It will be difficult to know when such a "war" ends. Comparing Pearl Harbor to September 11 may be politically helpful, but the analogy is rather weak.

Let's look at one more completely different example of a weak analogy generated by T. Edward Damer (*Attacking Faulty Reasoning*, Third edition, Belmont, CA: Wadsworth 1995, p. 102):

> *If one were to listen to only one kind of music or eat only one kind of food, it would soon become tasteless and boring. Variety makes eating and listening exciting and enriching experiences. Therefore, it could be concluded that an exclusive sexual relationship with only one member of the opposite sex for the rest of one's life--that is, marriage--does not hold out much hope for very much excitement or enrichment.*

Although this argument might have some logic on the surface, it ultimately fails because the comparison is weak. Food and music cannot fairly be compared to a complex human relationship. The consequences of eating different types of food and listening to different types of music are very dissimilar to the consequences of having many sexual relationships with many different people!

It is easy to be misled by faulty analogies. Many of these analogies are reasonable, to a point. But they often have significant differences which make them break down under scrutiny. They are simple on the surface, but complex underneath. Misleading advertisers and arguers often rely on them because they catch uncritical thinkers off guard and seem plausible.

Errors Based on Emotion

It is easy, as we discussed in Chapter 1, to confuse our feelings with our thinking. As human beings, we are highly susceptible to our emotions which can sometimes cloud the clarity of our thinking. This can come in the form of one of the two following errors:

- Resisting Change/Appeal to Tradition
- Direct Appeal to Emotion

Resisting Change/Appeal to Tradition

Nobody likes change. We are all accustomed to our routines and often dislike it when anything important in our life changes. This is a natural, emotional human tendency, but it can cause problems. When we reject an idea simply because it is new, we are not really considering its merits. We may, on some level, be afraid to change. We may be rejecting an idea that is good, but we will never know if we fail to honestly consider it.

Let's look at an example. Tom works for the electric company and has been working in the control room of a local power plant since his graduation from a community college three years ago. Until now, he has always worked under the direct supervision of an engineer. Today, his supervisor suggests that he is ready to work more independently, handling the controls by himself for a few hours each day, while his supervisor catches up on some paperwork in an adjoining office. Tom's first reaction is swift and clear: he's not interested. "I'm not able to handle this amount of responsibility, and I'm not paid enough either," he tells his supervisor.

Tom's reaction was quick and probably emotional. He rejected the idea without really considering it fairly. He was more than likely afraid of the new level of responsibility, and he was uncomfortable changing his job. Nevertheless, his supervisor suggested he think about it for a few days before deciding. As Tom thought about the offer, he gradually began to see some good in it. He was pleased his supervisor thought he could handle it, and maybe he could. Besides, the supervisor would still be available if he got into trouble. Tom also thought it would be a challenge to assume a new responsibility. The next day, he told his supervisor he'd take the job. Tom had a chance to think about the new job and had changed his mind. When he applied some critical thinking skills to the problem, he was able to reach a rational conclusion.

Even good thinkers have a tendency to react negatively to new ideas. The good thinker recognizes this tendency, puts her emotions aside and considers the problem rationally before making a decision. A poor thinker will react quickly and reject new or unfamiliar ideas without careful consideration.

Can you think of a time when you have rejected an idea or plan simply because it was new? More than likely you can. Can you think of a change that you initially thought would be negative but which turned out to be a good thing? The lesson is simple: don't reject an idea without evaluating it thoughtfully. Consider it carefully, applying your critical thinking skills before you make a decision. You may find that the idea is a bad one. If so, reject it, but don't reject it before you have fairly examined it.

Sometimes arguers will appeal to tradition to suggest that change is not good nor necessary. It is possible that the change proposed is not reasonable. But if that is so, an argument should be made as to why it's unreasonable. Just arguing that we should always keep things as they have been, while offering no evidence, is itself unreasonable.

Whenever we hear someone argue that there's no need to change something because "We've been doing it that way for years," this is an appeal to tradition. Some people oppose many types of educational reform for this reason. To suggest that we should avoid changing the way we teach reading in the schools simply because we've been successful teaching reading the old way is an appeal to tradition. It may be that the new way is not effective, but if this is true, it should be rejected on its own merits, not just because it is new.

Another example would be arguing that we don't need any form of gun registration because we have never needed it in the past. It is possible that circumstances have changed now, making gun registration necessary. It is also possible that it is not necessary. But arguing that it is not a good idea because we've never had it before is appealing to tradition.

Direct Appeal to Emotion

This fallacy occurs when an arguer appeals directly to emotion rather than logic to make a point. It can be very effective to appeal to emotions because they are such powerful motivators. Advertisers know this and use these appeals regularly. The problem is that we cannot think clearly when we are reacting with our emotions. We may make decisions we would not otherwise make. The emotions most commonly used are pity and fear. Consider these examples:

From a television ad... "You can help this starving child. [Camera shows a beautiful, but dirty child, dressed in rags, looking wide-eyed at the camera.] For just pennies a day, you can help feed this child and make a difference in her life. " It is difficult to resist such an appeal, but we are not provided with enough information. How much of the money I donate will go to this child? Does anyone profit from this program? Are there similar programs that provide more effective help for this child. If we react only with our emotions, we don't ask these difficult questions.

From a political commercial... "If you vote for the gay rights ordinance, gays will have special rights. The next thing you know, they'll be taking over the schools and advocating homosexuality in the classroom. Is this what you want?" In this case, the speaker is appealing to the audience's fear of having children being influenced by homosexuals advocating the gay lifestyle. There is no evidence given that this ordinance would enable this to occur. The appeal is strictly emotional.

Of course, appeals to emotion are effective, which is why advertisers regularly appeal to our fear, greed, or vanity. We are all emotional creatures and so are susceptible to these types of appeals. Clear thinkers, however, can easily recognize when an argument is using an emotional appeal and consider the case on its rational merits. Often, no rational argument is offered. It is easier to get people to react emotionally. If they think clearly about what they are doing, they might not think it's such a good idea!

Errors of Evasion

Errors of evasion are fairly straightforward. The errors are often used when people are uncomfortable addressing an issue directly. They are often used in political advertisements and in editorial arguments. They include the following:

- Attacking the Person
- Red Herring
- Straw Man

Attacking the Person (Ad Hominem)

One of the most common ways to avoid addressing a logical point is to shift the discussion towards the person instead of his ideas. We see this most commonly in political campaigns. When candidates run negative television ads criticizing their opponents, they are engaging in ad hominem tactics. These ads usually impugn the character of their political opponents, thus diverting attention from the issues of the campaign that they'd prefer not to address.

To use a general example, negative political ads often accuse an opponent of changing his mind, and his positions on issues. They depict this "flip flopping" as a weakness, a sure sign that the candidate has no principles. In fact, as we have discussed in Chapter 2, sometimes the most reasonable response is to change one's mind, especially if circumstances have changed. The candidate who focuses on the "character flaws" of an opponent is avoiding discussion of the issues themselves.

Everyone sometimes has a tendency to fall into this trap. It is often easier to attack the person than to respond to an issue directly. If a student claims that the grade she received in a course was not fair because the professor disliked her and showed favoritism toward other students, she would be committing an ad hominem fallacy. She should present evidence supporting her claim that the grade was unfair rather than attacking the professor personally.

Red Herring

Think of a red herring as a "stinky fish." When someone throws a stinky fish into a conversation, everyone is likely to forget what they were discussing and notice the smell. Similarly, a red herring is an irrelevant claim that is introduced into an argument to distract the listener or reader from the issue at hand. It is commonly used when one wants to change the subject to avoid addressing the relevant issue.

I remember my children, as teenagers, using this fallacy frequently:

"How did you do on the math test, today."
"Well... Dad... you need to understand that NOBODY did well on that test..."

Of course, how everyone else did is irrelevant to the original question.

In the context of an argument, red herrings are common. Consider the following argument:

> We should not legalize marijuana for medical use. We already provide the ingredients of marijuana in prescription form for patients who need it, so it is not necessary for us to make it legal. Furthermore, we are making headway in our war against drugs. Teenagers often start with marijuana and then move on to more deadly drugs like cocaine and heroin!

In this case, the writer uses a red herring by suggesting that teens who start with marijuana will move on to other drugs. This is irrelevant to the issue of providing marijuana for medical use.

Politicians when asked a question they would prefer not to answer often employ a red herring:

> Question: Did you support a bill to cut federal funding to education?

> Answer: Are you questioning my commitment to education? Did you know I used to be a teacher? I have always been committed to education.

He has not answered the question, preferring to use a red herring.

Straw Man

Just like a scarecrow is a fake person, a straw man is a fake argument. Let's look at an example. Suppose you have a teenage daughter. She is sixteen and loves going out with her friends at night. Being a responsible parent, you suggest that she should have a curfew of midnight. Her response is perhaps predictable. "Midnight??!! Why do you want to control every aspect of my life. You want to take away all my freedom!" She has taken your original statement and modified it to make it sound unreasonable. Simply suggesting a midnight curfew became a boldfaced attempt to control her entire life. This is a straw man: a shifting of an opponent's argument so it's more unreasonable and easier to attack.

A straw man is used when someone does not want to, or cannot, respond directly to a specific position, so they change the opposing position so it's no longer the same position and easier to respond to. They have inserted a "straw man" into the discussion.

Predictably, the straw man occurs in negative campaign commercials. Let's presume candidate A has suggested that we spend more money to strengthen immigration enforcement to identify and prevent undesirable or dangerous illegal immigrants from entering the United States. Candidate B, who is running against Candidate A in a college town, could misrepresent Candidate A's position by claiming," Candidate A would like to stop any foreign nationals from getting student visas to study in the U.S." This is a classic straw man, which will likely appeal to many student voters, but it misrepresents Candidate A's position.

Let's consider another example:

Candidate A: "I am not opposed to raising some revenue to balance the budget."

Candidate B: "Candidate A says she is in favor of raising some revenue to balance the budget. Middle class taxpayers like you already pay too much in taxes! My opponent obviously wants to stick it to you again. This just is not fair! "

Candidate A has claimed he is in favor of raising revenues, not necessarily raising taxes on the middle class like Candidate B claims. Therefore, Candidate B is using a straw man because he is misrepresenting Candidate A's position.

In the 1970's an Equal Rights Amendment was proposed for the U. S. Constitution making it unconstitutional to discriminate on the basis of gender. The amendment, to pass, had to be ratified by two-thirds of the states' legislatures, or thirty-four states. It was quickly passed by most of the thirty-four states; then it ran into trouble. The opponents, using a classic straw man (or straw woman?) claimed that what the supporters were trying to accomplish was to create a "unisex" society where there could be no legal distinction between men and women. There would be , they claimed, no more single sex public restrooms or separate boys and girls locker rooms in schools. These claims, although untrue, scared many people to the point where state legislatures began to rescind their previous support for the amendment. The straw man was effective, and the ERA never passed.

Perhaps you can think of some examples when the opponents of an idea misrepresented the idea to generate opposition to it. It occurs frequently, and can be effective, but a good thinker will recognize the tactic as fallacious.

Exercise 3.1

Think of a time in your life when you made one of the thinking errors based on *insufficient evidence.* Explain the situation and explain which type of evidence error it was.

Exercise 3.2

Think of a time in your life when you made one of the thinking errors based on *oversimplification.* Explain the situation and explain which type of oversimplification error it was.

Exercise 3.3

Think of a time in your life when you made one of the thinking errors based on *emotion.* Explain the situation and explain the error.

Exercise 3.4

Try to remember an example of one of the errors based on evasion. Your example could be a political ad, an argument you've heard people repeat, or even a strategy you've used yourself. Describe the example and explain which type of evasion error was used.

Exercise 3.5

Think of a popular issue you think many people tend to oversimplify. Describe the issue and explain why you think people tend to oversimplify it. In what ways is the issue actually more complex? Does this example fit into any of the oversimplification errors discussed in this chapter?

Exercise 3.6

Find, or try to remember, a political advertisement that uses fallacious thinking to make its point. Describe the advertisement and explain which ad or fallacy the ad uses.

Exercise 3.7

IDENTIFY and EXPLAIN each of the following errors based on *insufficient evidence* or *oversimplification*.

1) I am going to oppose the gay rights ordinance. The proponents claim it will prevent discrimination in housing, employment, and lodging. I don't personally know any gay or lesbian people who have suffered from discrimination. Therefore, I don't think such an ordinance in necessary.

2) I love eating in Asian restaurants. Asian people are so polite and friendly.

3) At the beginning of the 1990 Iraq War, over eighty percent of the American public supported the war effort and thought it was justified. That many people are not likely wrong.

4) Our son's little league team needs to get a better coach. They need to decide if they're serious about winning or not. Otherwise, they should just keep the present coach and be satisfied with losing.

5) Colleges that charge more tuition provide a better education. After all, you get what you pay for.

6) I know Jill cheated. She sat next to Carole and got the same answers wrong!

7) We should allow prayers back into the schools. It has overwhelming support in the community, where, in a recent poll, sixty-five percent of the people want their children to pray in school.

8) Doing homework is like any other chore. Set aside some time for it every day and it shouldn't take too long to do.

9) My son wants to sell used cars. I really think he could find a more respectable profession.

10) That damn mechanic! I had him fix my brakes last week and today my front wheel started making a loud noise.

11) Children need to be trained with consistent discipline, not unlike how we train purebred dogs. We reward dogs for proper behavior, and they behave. It's really no different for children. It's about consistent discipline.

12) Critical thinking instruction should be required of every student graduating from high school. It's clear that all high school graduates should be able to think critically.

13) The schools need cleaning up. Since they started assigning *Catcher in the Rye* in the English classes, drug and alcohol abuse have gone up. We have to get that book off the shelves.

14) We need to invest in more computers for this college. An article in this week's *Chronicle of Higher Education* claimed that successful education increasingly will depend on students' access to technology.

15) Parents ought to be held legally liable for vandalism caused by their children. After all, parents are ultimately responsible for their children's behavior.

Exercise 3.8

IDENTIFY and EXPLAIN each of the following errors based on *emotion* or *evasion*.

1) I don't think John's proposal is a good one. After all, he showed up for his presentation dressed in blue jeans and a T-shirt. He has no credibility as far as I'm concerned.

2) Susan thinks we should reconsider the school calendar for next year. I don't know about you, but I think going to school all summer is a ridiculous idea. I am going to oppose Susan.

3) Do you actually want to permit this child with AIDS to be in your child's classroom? Think about it. Are you willing to take the risk?

4) June thinks men should be put in jail if they don't pay child support. If she had it her way, men would have no legal rights at all. She's being so unreasonable.

5) You say I cheated on this exam? Are you aware of how much cheating goes on at this college? It's everywhere! Open your eyes.

6) My son says he needs a laptop for college. When we were in college, we used the computer cluster in the library. It was fine for us, and it didn't cost anything.

7) We should pass a constitutional amendment allowing prayer in public schools. Until the Supreme Court declared such prayer unconstitutional, children prayed every day in school, for many years, without a problem. What's the harm?

8) By arguing in favor of registration of handguns, you are really arguing for the eventual banning of private gun ownership. THAT is simply unacceptable because the U.S. Constitution guarantees our right to bear arms.

9) She would not make a good manager in our company. She can't even discipline her own children!

10) Are you in favor of cutting welfare benefits? Do you realize this will likely lead to less money for single moms with children? Who will be responsible for sending these children to bed hungry?

11) The president wants to cut taxes on capital gains because he obviously wants to put more money in the hands of those who are already rich. He clearly favors his own kind.

12) Have I ever taken a campaign donation from a tobacco company? I'll tell you what, my opponents have taken money from beer companies. Alcohol is a major problem in this country.

13) I really disagreed with George W. Bush's tax policies. He couldn't even explain them clearly. Whenever he tried to, he would always misspeak.

14) You ask if I support more funds for Social Security? Let me tell you, my mother is ninety-two years old. Do you think I would do anything to hurt her?

CHAPTER 4
The Elements of an Argument

During an average day, we are bombarded by messages from many sources. Advertisers ask us to buy their products. Politicians ask for our votes. Our loved ones try to convince us their point of view is correct. Coworkers present proposals to us for consideration. Various groups try to convince us to accept their ideas on abortion, gun control, smoking, and countless other issues. Each time we are the target of such persuasion, we are being asked to consider an **argument**.

We may commonly think of an argument as a verbal competition between two people, often loud and rarely solving anything. In critical thinking, we use the term argument to refer to the process of presenting a particular position on an issue, trying to convince the readers or listeners that one point of view is the most reasonable. We construct our own arguments every day, as we also consider the arguments of others. In this chapter, we will consider how to identify an argument, what its parts are, and how to diagram it so we can analyze it.

One place we see a lot of arguments is the editorial page of a newspaper. Here we read editorials written by the editors of the newspaper, op-ed pieces by contributors, and letters to the editor written by readers. These are often arguments: they are written to try to persuade us to believe a particular point of view. The authors might write to support a particular candidate for office or to express their opinion about some problem or proposal being debated in the community. These are good examples of the kind of arguments we see regularly. Of course, not all articles or letters to the editor are arguments. Sometimes people write to thank someone for a job well done or to notify the readers of some upcoming community event. In these cases, the writers are not trying necessarily to convince us to believe their point of view. They might just be informing us about something.

As critical thinkers, we need to be able to recognize arguments. As we read a letter or another written piece, we need to decide whether or not the writer is, first and foremost, trying to convince us to believe or to do something. If this is the case, we are reading an argument. It may not be an effective argument, but its purpose is to argue a point.

We need to keep in mind that, as we've discussed earlier, reasonable people can disagree about complicated issues. Let's assume we read an argument prepared by someone who has a particular point of view on an issue of concern to us. That person will be presenting the most reasonable argument possible to persuade us that the view is correct. If the argument is well constructed, we may be impressed and likely to accept the reasoning. Nevertheless, if an equally competent arguer presented a well-constructed argument advocating an opposing view on the same subject, we might also be impressed with that logic. Just because an arguer presents a well-reasoned argument, it does not necessarily follow that the position is correct. Equally effective arguments can be constructed to advocate opposing viewpoints. It is up to us, as critical thinkers, to carefully consider all arguments before deciding which one we agree with. This is the purpose of arguments: to present logical reasons for accepting one point of view, which other thinkers can consider when making up their minds.

It's important to remember that we will read and hear many weak arguments as well as well-constructed ones. Sometimes weak arguments appear better than they are because we are likely to react emotionally to them or tend to agree with them from the beginning. A good critical thinker can recognize a weak argument, even if she agrees with the writer's conclusion. Conversely, she should be able to recognize a well-constructed argument, even if it is presenting a point of view in opposition to her own.

The Components of an Argument

The purpose of an argument is to convince the reader that a particular statement is correct. This statement presents the point of view of the arguer and is called the **conclusion** or **claim** of the argument. The arguer presents **reasons** or **premises** as evidence for the conclusion. When we analyze an argument, we must first identify the conclusion and the reasons the arguer presents as evidence for the conclusion.

In diagram form, the components of an argument can be presented like this:

> **Reason**
> **Reason**
> **Reason**
> +**Reason**
> **Conclusion**

The first step in evaluating the quality of an argument is to identify its conclusion and supporting reasons. In other words, we cannot begin to decide whether the argument is well reasoned until we first figure out what it is the writer is arguing. We need to be careful not to start reacting to the author's points until we have first diagrammed the argument. To do this, we must identify the conclusion.

Identifying the Conclusion

A clearly written argument will have an identifiable conclusion:

> **Although most parents care deeply about their children, some situations occur when children are put at great risk by remaining in the home. If parents are beating, sexually abusing, or even neglecting their children, the children could be considered in jeopardy. In these cases, the children could have a better chance to grow up in a healthy environment if they were placed in a foster home. Yes, there are**

circumstances when children ought to be removed from their parents' home.

In this argument, the conclusion is quite clearly stated in the last sentence:

> There are circumstances when children ought to be removed from their parents' home.

The conclusion does not always appear at the end of the argument:

> I would agree that many families exhibit violent, even abusive behavior. But this must be considered in the context of the society in which we live. Violence is all around us and can be expected to show up in family dynamics. The bottom line, however, is that most families love their children. Children belong with their parents and should not be removed from the home. The harm caused by forcibly removing a child from the home may be worse than any problem the child may suffer while remaining in the home. Besides, abuse also can occur in foster homes.

In this case, the conclusion appears in the middle of the argument:

> Children...should not be removed from the home.

Sometimes, the conclusion is not directly stated in the argument and needs to be supplied by the reader:

> Imagine how it would feel to dedicate your life to serving the needs of the sick and the frail, only to find out that your efforts were rewarded with the AIDS virus (HIV). Health care workers are exposed to HIV everyday, and they have no way of knowing who has it. They are exposed to patients' body fluids all the time, putting themselves in danger of contracting the virus. If they knew a patient was HIV positive, they could exercise more caution, but they would still treat the patient. Health care workers deserve to know. Why are they blocked from testing all incoming patients for HIV? It makes no sense.

In this case, the conclusion is fairly obvious, even though it is not directly stated: Patients should routinely be tested for HIV.

Conclusions can be tricky to find, especially if the argument is not well written:

> I'm sick and tired of the politicians who want to pamper the prisoners. If they want toothpaste, they should have thought about that when they committed their crimes. I can't afford to pay enough taxes to

keep these creeps in the lap of luxury while I work hard to keep food on the table. This is why the public always refuses to build more prisons. Schools alone are costing us enough, and they are not even doing the job. The other day, I heard about prisoners in California who were complaining because they didn't have cable TV. Can you imagine?

This is obviously not a well-written argument. The writer brings up several issues, but if we were to give it our best guess, the writer's conclusion is probably something like this: **Prisoners should not be given unnecessary luxuries at taxpayers' expense.**

Finding the conclusion may be difficult. We may think there is more than one conclusion. Consider this argument:

Once again we have read about a young person who has taken out his rage on his fellow students by bringing firearms into school and randomly shooting innocent people. In the most recent example, the shooter took the guns from his father's gun case. Clearly, having access to these guns at home contributed to the tragedy. We need to make parents legally responsible for any firearms they own. Shooters also get guns from gun shows where people can buy guns without adequate background checks. We need to pass legislation to prevent this. In other words, we simply need to do more to protect our schoolchildren from gun violence!

In this argument, the arguer seems to be arguing two points: that parents should be held legally liable for crimes committed with their guns, and that people should not be able to buy guns at gun shows without background checks. In fact, the last sentence of the passage could suggest a wider conclusion: **We need to do more to protect our schoolchildren from gun violence.** We need to pass a number of new laws to reduce gun violence, including parental responsibility AND background checks for guns purchased at gun shows. The conclusion should include the widest possible point made in the argument.

If you have difficulty identifying the conclusion in an argument, ask yourself the following questions: What is the "bottom line?" What point is the writer making? If I take everything else away, what does the writer want me to believe? The answer to that question is the conclusion. If you cannot answer that question, it could mean that the passage you are reading is not really an argument. It could also mean that the argument is not very well written. In any case, you cannot proceed with your analysis of the argument until you identify the conclusion. Then you need to figure out what statements the author is making to support the conclusion. These are the reasons.

Identifying the Reasons

The reasons present the heart of the argument. **Reasons are statements the arguer uses to convince us that the conclusion is true.** Stating the conclusion, by itself, does not convince us of anything. If the reasons are acceptable and persuasive, and if there are enough of them to suggest that the conclusion is true, then the argument is effective. So, after we have identified the conclusion in the argument, we must next identify and isolate the reasons.

Just as with the conclusion, the reasons are not always easy to find. Sometimes we must do our best to determine the reasons, even if the arguer has not made the reasons as explicit as we would like. Let's take another look at our first sample argument:

> **Although most parents care deeply about their children, some situations occur when children are put at great risk by remaining in the home. If parents are beating, sexually abusing, or even neglecting their children, the children could be considered in jeopardy. In these cases, the children could have a better chance to grow up in a healthy environment if they were placed in a foster home. Yes, there are circumstances when children ought to be removed from their parents' home.**

We have already determined that the last sentence presents the conclusion, but what are the reasons? Not all statements in the argument can be considered reasons. The two reasons given in the above argument might be stated as follows:

Children are sometimes at risk in their homes.
   [Examples: beating, sexual abuse, neglect]

Such children would have a better chance to grow up in a healthy environment if they were placed in a foster home.

Notice that the first reason is not stated directly in the argument. It is, rather, the main idea presented in the first sentence. The second sentence presents **examples** of the types of situations that may result in risk. This helps the arguer make the meaning clear. But the second sentence does not present another reason; it supports the first reason. The third sentence presents the second reason.

When we diagram an argument, we will present the conclusions and reasons as follows:

R1: Children are sometimes at risk in their homes.

   SR1: Some examples include beating, sexual abuse, and neglect.

61

R2: Such children would have a better chance to grow up in a healthy environment if they were placed in a foster home.

C: There are circumstances when children ought to be removed from their parents' home.

Notice that the examples that support the first reason are listed as a subreason of R1. It is common to find subreasons that actually support other reasons rather than the conclusion.

Let's look at our second example:

> I would agree that many families exhibit violent, even abusive behavior. But this must be considered in the context of the society in which we live. Violence is all around us and can be expected to show up in family dynamics. The bottom line, however, is that most families love their children. Children belong with their parents, and should not be removed from the home. The harm caused by removing a child from the home may be worse than any problem the child may suffer while remaining in the home. Besides, abuse also can occur in foster homes.

> The reasoning in this argument could be diagrammed as follows:

R1: The violence in society sometimes shows up in families.

R2: Most parents love their children.

R3: The harm caused by forcibly removing a child from the home may be worse than any problem the child may suffer while remaining in the home.

R4: Abuse also can occur in foster homes.

C: Children should not be removed from the home.

Notice that the first two reasons were paraphrased from the original wording, while the last two could be taken word for word from the argument. If the wording of the reason is clear and concise, then copy the exact words when diagramming the argument. If the wording is longer, gives examples, or is repetitive, then paraphrase the reason. The purpose of diagramming is to present the argument in a concise, easy-to-read format, but be careful not to change the meaning of the reasons when you construct the diagram. Sometimes, we have to use our best estimate of the reasons and conclusion, as we see in our third example:

> Imagine how it would feel to dedicate your life to serving the needs of the sick and the frail, only to find out that your efforts were rewarded with the AIDS virus (HIV). Health care workers are exposed to HIV

everyday, and they have no way of knowing who has it. They are exposed to patients' body fluids all the time, putting themselves in danger of contracting the virus. If they knew a patient was HIV positive, they could exercise more caution, but they would still treat the patient. Health care workers deserve to know. Why are they blocked from testing all incoming patients for HIV? It makes no sense.

R1: Health care workers are exposed to HIV by their exposure to body fluids.

R2: Health care workers do not know who has HIV because they are prevented from testing patients.

R3: If health care workers knew which patients had HIV, they could exercise more caution while treating these patients.

C: Patients should routinely be tested for HIV.

In this argument, the reasons were not stated in a usable form, so we had to reword the reasons so they could be examined closely. Again, it is important to remember that our purpose in diagramming the argument is to help us examine its logic. Sometimes, the way the argument is written, we have to make the best approximation of the arguer's meaning in order to diagram the argument. In these cases, we cannot always be sure of the arguer's intent, but we must do the best we can. Let's take another look at the following argument:

> I'm sick and tired of the politicians who want to pamper the prisoners. If they want toothpaste, they should have thought about that when they committed their crimes. I can't afford to pay enough taxes to keep these creeps in the lap of luxury while I work hard to keep food on the table. This is why the public always refuses to build more prisons. Schools alone are costing us enough, and they are not even doing the job. The other day, I heard about prisoners in California who were complaining because they didn't have cable TV. Can you imagine?

R1: Taxpayers can't afford to pay for luxuries, like toothpaste and cable TV, for prisoners.

R2: Taxpayers don't vote to build more prisons because the prisons provide such luxuries.

R3: Schools are expensive for taxpayers, and they are not effective.

C: Prisoners should not be given unnecessary luxuries at taxpayers' expense.

In this example, we have to do our best to diagram the author's reasoning, even though we cannot be sure we are correct. When the person wrote this letter to the editor, he was not aware of how to write a clear argument, so his letter is not as clear as it otherwise might be. In practice, arguments come in all varieties and levels of excellence. If all arguments were carefully written with a list of reasons and an explicit conclusion, they would be easier to examine. Because they are not, we must do our best to approximate the original intent of the arguer.

Let's take a look at our final example:

> Once again we have read about a young person who has taken out his rage on his fellow students by bringing firearms into school and randomly shooting innocent people. In the most recent example, the shooter took the guns from his father's gun case. Clearly, having access to these guns at home contributed to the tragedy. We need to make parents legally responsible for any firearms they own. Shooters also get guns from gun shows where people can buy guns without adequate background checks. We need to pass legislation to prevent this. In other words, we simply need to do more to protect our schoolchildren from gun violence!

R1: We need to make parents legally responsible for the firearms they own.

> SR1: In the most recent school shooting, the shooter took the gun from his father's gun case.

R2: We need to do background checks on people who buy guns at gun shows.

> SR1: Shooters sometimes buy their weapons at gun shows.

C: We can do more to protect our schoolchildren from gun violence.

An important point to remember about diagramming the argument: our purpose is to present the argument the way the arguer presented it, not the way we think it would be most effective. We are trying to see if the argument is an effective one. When we list the reasons, we must list the reasons the arguer presented, even if we think they are poor or irrelevant. After we have identified the reasons, we can evaluate them. In the above examples, some of the reasons are obviously weak, which we would later point out if we were to complete our evaluation of this argument.

After we have diagrammed an argument, isolated the arguer's reasons and conclusions, we need to examine the reasons to start to determine whether the argument is an effective one. We will be examining this process in the next three chapters and in the appendix.

In the following exercises, DIAGRAM the arguments:

4.1 No matter how much money we put into eliminating prostitution, it will never be effective. Women and men will always be willing to sell their bodies for sex, and people will always pay for prostitutes. Also, as long as prostitution is illegal, we will have the problem of street crime associated with prostitution. We might think prostitution is wrong, but legalization of prostitution makes sense. It won't eliminate all the problems, but it will enable us to face the problem realistically.

4.2 People who dub CD's from friends are not doing anything wrong. First of all, they probably would not have bought the CD anyway, so the artist is not losing any money. Also, the record companies raise their prices to account for people making copies of their CD's. Besides, the practice of copying CD's goes on all the time, and everyone knows it.

4.3 I am so sick of coupons. I think manufacturers should get rid of them. They are a pain to use. You have to cut them out and sort them, which takes lots of time. Then when you use them, it holds up the grocery line. It costs the stores lots of money to sort and send them back. In fact, I heard that coupons raise the cost of items in the grocery stores by 30%.

4.4 I am glad the state now requires all children to be buckled in when they are riding in passenger cars. I always buckle up my children when they go in the car with me. What I wonder is why don't we require the children to be buckled in when they ride in school buses? It would seem to be the same thing. I knew a coworker who had two small children who were not buckled in when she took them to school. She was in an accident, and both children suffered severe head injuries. The same thing could happen on a bus. Some would say it is very expensive to install seat belts on buses, but wouldn't one life saved be worth the cost?

4.5 Many think that cell phones cause car accidents. Although this is sometimes true, I am not in favor of banning them while driving, as lawmakers have proposed. Requiring drivers to pull off the road to talk on the cell phone is dangerous; we'd have people pulling over everywhere. This could cause accidents too! Lots of activities cause drivers to get distracted: eating, fiddling with the radio, and tending children, just to name a few. Why single out cell phones? Cell phones can also do something useful, like report accidents or drunken drivers.

CHAPTER 5
Clarity versus Ambiguity

Ambiguity in Arguments

Many arguments fail because they contain language that is not clear. Language itself is inherently vague. Words have multiple meanings, and it is not always clear from the context of a statement exactly what the writer means. Let's look at an example adapted from a letter to the editor:

> **I'm getting sick and tired of professionals who rip off the public every day. It's time we took a stand and put a stop to this.**

The language used in this statement is not clear. Its meaning is not precise enough to be of any value. The word "professionals" is ambiguous. It could mean any number of things. For example, it could refer to particular job titles, like lawyers or physicians. It could include other professions as well, perhaps car salespeople, business owners, or exterminators. Perhaps, from the context, we could interpret it to mean expert con artists who manage to find effective ways to steal people's money.

We also do not know what the writer means by "rip off." It obviously refers to cheating or otherwise being dishonest to take people's money, but it is not precise. Perhaps if we knew what "professionals" the author was talking about we could identify a more precise meaning for the words "rip off."

Let's consider another example. The following statement recently appeared in a political advertisement:

> **So elect me this November. Together we can make America safe again.**

So what does this mean? It sounds good. Who wouldn't want to make America safe? But HOW would this happen? In order to understand this statement, we need to know in what ways the candidate now considers America to be unsafe. She could be referring to crime, that the streets are unsafe because of the danger of being robbed or murdered. She could be referring to natural disasters, inferring that we are not prepared for tornadoes or hurricanes. She could also be referring to threats to our health or to workplace accidents. The fact is, we might be able to figure out generally what the candidate meant by hearing the statement in context. Let's assume the candidate had just made reference to a recent school shooting. We might then presume that the candidate was referring to making America safe from gun violence. But even if we knew this, we would not know HOW the candidate would protect us from this. Therefore, we do not have enough information to decide whether or not this is a good reason to vote for the candidate.

Let's examine how ambiguity affects the quality of an argument. When we have identified the reasons and conclusion in an argument, we need to be able to determine if the reasons are, themselves, acceptable statements. To evaluate this, we must first be able to assign a precise, unambiguous meaning to the reason.

Consider the following argument adapted from a recent letter to the editor urging voters to support a local candidate for election to the state legislature:

> I am writing to urge all residents of the district to support the candidacy of David Schneider. During his first two terms in office, David has demonstrated that he is a strong and capable leader. He served the residents of this district with integrity and dedication. Since he has been in Albany, he has learned who the movers and the shakers are, and we need someone who can hit the ground running.

We might diagram this argument as follows:

R1: David Schneider has demonstrated that he is a strong and capable leader during his first two terms.

R2: He has served the residents of this district with integrity and dedication.

R3: We need a candidate who can hit the ground running.
 SR1: He has learned who the movers and shakers are in Albany
 [so he will not have to learn this from scratch].

C: Re-elect David Schneider

Our first step in evaluating the quality of an argument is to consider each reason separately. To do this, we must first determine whether each reason is an acceptable statement. In other words, is the reason likely to be a true statement? If all the reasons are acceptable and relevant to the conclusion, then we have the makings of an effective argument.

Let's look at the reasons in this argument. The problem we immediately run into is one of ambiguity. None of the reasons have clear, unambiguous meanings. In reason one, the ambiguous words are "strong, capable leader." What does it mean to be a strong and capable leader? It sounds good but means little by itself. The reason would be far better had the writer explained in more detail what this phrase means. In reason two, the ambiguous phrase is "served ...with integrity and dedication." Once again, we do not know exactly what this means. If the writer had used some examples of what Schneider did to demonstrate that he served with integrity and with dedication, we might understand more precisely what the reason means. The third reason is a bit clearer. Although the phrase "hit the ground running" is somewhat vague, from the context of the argument and from the subreason, we can tell that the author means that David will be able to immediately get down to work without having to learn as much as a newcomer would. Nevertheless, there is still some significant ambiguity. What or who are the "movers and shakers"? Presumably, these are powerful political leaders, but are they legislative leaders, lobbyists, business leaders, or who? And how will the fact that David knows these people enable him to be more effective? Much of this is left up to the reader. To be effective, all the reasons, at a minimum, need to be clear, unambiguous statements. This argument fails on this criterion alone.

Sometimes the conclusion, or claim, itself is ambiguous. Take the following argument about drunk driving:

> More than thirty-five people died on Maine's roads last year as a result of drunk driving, according to the State Police report. All the efforts we are making to reduce this problem are not showing the results we had hoped for. The local chapter of Mothers Against Drunk Driving has suggested that the penalties are still not strict enough. Others have suggested that the laws prohibiting drunk driving are severe enough, but they are not being enforced. We simply need to get serious about this problem, once and for all.

We might diagram the argument as follows:

> R1: According to the state police, more than thirty-five people died last year in drunk driving accidents in Maine.
>
> R2: All the efforts we've made to reduce drunk driving have been ineffective.
>
>> SR1: According to MADD, penalties are not severe enough.
>>
>> SR2: Some believe the laws are strict enough but are not being enforced.
>>
>> C: We need to get serious about preventing drunk driving.

In this example, it is the conclusion itself that is unclear. What does it mean to "get serious" about this problem? From the context, it could mean that we need stricter penalties. It could also mean that we need to enforce the existing penalties. Or it could mean something altogether different. We cannot evaluate an argument that has been written to prove a claim, if the claim itself is not clear.

As we have seen, ambiguity can make an argument ineffective. We cannot evaluate something if we do not understand exactly what it means. For this reason, we need to be able to identify ambiguous words or phrases in an argument. Actually, ambiguity comes in several forms, and we need to be on the lookout for all of them.

Types of Ambiguity

Perhaps the most common type of ambiguity is words or phrases that are so general that they have no precise meaning. We sometimes refer to this as **vagueness**. A word that is vague is often very abstract or general. For example, if Susan told you that she interviewed a candidate for the new position who *is head and shoulders above the rest*, she would not be conveying a precise meaning. Susan obviously believes that this is a superior candidate, but the phrase she uses to describe him is vague. It doesn't suggest WHY she thinks he was the best candidate. It could be because of his experience, his communication skills, his motivation, or any number of other possibilities. It could, if taken literally, refer to his height, but this is unlikely from the context.

Other examples of vague statements include the meaningless words often used in advertising claims. A recent automobile ad claimed that their automobile was so technologically advanced that it provided a "*seamless bond between you and the road.*" What does that mean? Taken literally, I'm not sure we would want to have a seamless bond between ourselves and the road! But even in the context of the ad, its meaning is obscure.

In some cases of ambiguity, the possible meanings for the words are not as wide open as in these examples. Often, an ambiguous word or phrase has only a limited number of reasonable interpretations, perhaps just two. Take the following as an example: *The use of manufacturing coupons causes people to have to spend too much time sorting them out, often just to realize a savings of only a few cents. This does not seem fair.* What, exactly, is the author claiming is unfair: having to spend all that time OR only saving a small amount of money OR a combination of the two? Any of those interpretations would be reasonable.

Let's consider another example:

> I am against capital punishment because our legal system is flawed. The laws of evidence can exclude information that might prove someone not guilty. Sometimes the wrong person is convicted of a crime. The possibility exists that an innocent person will be convicted and executed. Therefore, I cannot support an irrevocable penalty.

In this example, there is an ambiguity about the writer's primary objection to the death penalty. On one hand he suggests that the problem is the flawed legal system and its rules of evidence. If this were rectified, might we presume this person would drop his opposition to this penalty? Later in the statement, the writer suggests that his opposition is based on the fact that the penalty is irrevocable. Even if the legal system were not flawed, the death penalty would be irrevocable. So, as readers, we are left wondering whether the writer's opposition is based on the flawed evidence laws or the finality of the penalty itself, or both.

Another specific type of ambiguity is called **equivocation**. Equivocation involves shifting the definition of a word so that its meaning is no longer what we would normally think it to be. A modern, although sordid, example of this is when President Clinton stated "I have not had sexual relations with that woman, Monica Lewinsky." To most of us, the word "sexual relations" means some type of sexual contact, including the type the President did have with Ms. Lewinsky. But the President was using equivocation, limiting the definition of "sexual relations" only to sexual intercourse. As a result, he was intentionally misleading and creating ambiguity about the truth.

Equivocation can be used in arguments to create ambiguity, which can lead to misleading or confusing logic. Take the following argument as an example:

> **The legislature has proposed a bill guaranteeing the rights of gays and lesbians. This bill would make it illegal to refuse to serve a meal in a restaurant, fire a person from a job, or refuse to grant them accommodations solely because of their sexual preference. They say this is a civil rights issue. But why do we want to provide gays and lesbians with special rights? I do not think they deserve to receive preferential treatment. As a result, I am strongly opposed to this bill.**
>
> **R1: The legislature wants to pass a bill protecting gays and lesbians from being refused service, employment, or accommodations.**
>
> **R2: This would amount to giving these people special rights that others do not have, which I think is wrong.**
>
> **C: This gay rights bill should not pass.**

In this argument, the author is equivocating with the words "special rights." We all have rights as citizens, which include the rights included in this bill. By referring to these rights, later in the argument, as "special rights" the author is changing the meaning of these words to make it appear as though this law would afford special privileges to this minority group. This is not what the proposal states, so the equivocation is misleading.

We sometimes use ambiguity intentionally to avoid having to use words that have harsh or negative meanings. When someone has lost their temper and caused a scene, we might suggest that they are "having a bad day." When we refer to a crippled person, it would be more appropriate to refer to the individual as "a person with a disability." When we know that someone in our family is suffering from vomiting and diarrhea we might tell people they are "not feeling well." In each of these cases, we have substituted vague words intentionally to make it more palatable. These are called **euphemisms**. In everyday conversation, they are fine to use because we usually understand what the person means. However, if euphemisms appear in an argument, we need to be certain we understand their meaning.

Looking for Ambiguity

When evaluating arguments, it is very important to be able to identify ambiguity. Here are some guidelines to use to locate serious ambiguities in arguments:

1. **Concentrate your search for ambiguity to the important words in an argument.** There may be ambiguity in other areas, but it may not have much effect on the quality of the reasoning. For example, if, in an argument about abortion, the author states, "In the past, when abortion was illegal, many women received unsafe, unsanitary abortions which caused much death and injury." The phrase, "unsafe, unsanitary abortions" is somewhat ambiguous in this context. The writer probably means that illegal abortions were done by nonprofessionals in unsanitary conditions, but this should be clarified to make the reasoning clear. On the other hand, "In the past" is also ambiguous, but having a precise meaning for these terms is not necessary to understanding the reasoning.

2. **Ask yourself the simple question, "Do I understand what the author is trying to say?"** If you cannot paraphrase the author's idea, and be confident that you have accurately done so, then you have likely identified an ambiguity.

3. Similarly, **to determine if a word or phrase is ambiguous, ask yourself if there is more than one reasonable interpretation that could be made.** If there are two or more possible meanings, then the phrase is ambiguous.

4. Finally, **look elsewhere in the argument for some type of clarification.** Frequently, an author will use an ambiguous word or words, but then clarify it later in the argument. He may use examples or elaboration. For example, suppose the author of an argument on welfare reform has stated that "many types of welfare fraud cost the taxpayers millions of dollars a year. " Although the term "welfare fraud" is ambiguous, he may clarify this by giving examples: specific cases of fraudulent welfare claims. He might also use elaboration and explain what he means by welfare fraud, later in the argument. In some cases, the ambiguity will be cleared up as you continue to read the argument. Sometimes, a word, which might be ambiguous in isolation, will assume an obvious meaning in the context of a particular argument. For example, if you were to look at the word "chemical." This is a word that could have a broad range of meanings, and might even refer to a specific chemical. The word, by itself, is ambiguous. However, in the context of an article on "chemical abuse," it would be clear, from the context, that the word "chemical" refers to alcohol or illicit drugs.

In the following exercises, (1) DIAGRAM the arguments and (2) IDENTIFY and EXPLAIN any ambiguous words or phrases:

5.1 When I go to the supermarket, I am appalled by the large amount of meat that is displayed and sold every day. Meat is not a necessary part of our diet. Many people around the world survive quite well without eating one bit of meat. Meat is also unhealthy. How much disease would we prevent if we left meat entirely out of our diets? Finally, the production of meat is detrimental to our environment. Raising cattle for slaughter uses up huge amounts of resources that could be more efficiently used to grow vegetables.

5.2 Many so-called animal lovers have long been opposed to animal experimentation. They claim that animal research is unnecessarily torturing and killing defenseless animals. This is simply not true. Most medical experiments completed on animals are essential to the research being done. Without these well-planned and executed experiments, many medical questions would go unanswered and many people would die. In fact, last year alone, over 280,000 people benefited because of experiments on animals. Other experimentation methods, including computer models, are limited and ineffective. Furthermore, the animals used in these experiments are treated humanely, so no one needs to worry about the mistreatment of these animals.

5.3 I would like to write in support of the issue of physician-assisted suicide. To me, it is not right for a patient to have to suffer needlessly when we have the power to completely eliminate it. When a patient is suffering from terminal cancer, the pain is often unmanageable. In these circumstances, it would seem reasonable to help the patient die. There is also the issue of dignity. Don't patients have the right to preserve their dignity? Of course, I also think this should be practiced under strict guidelines. But in the final analysis, shouldn't the patient have the right to choose?

5.4 I think that the problem of sexual harassment has been overblown. It seems as though these days, people are afraid to say or do anything for fear it might be interpreted as sexual harassment. Males and females are different; let's face it. Men look at the world differently than women, and they need to be able to express their sexuality without worrying about who they might offend. Most of what people call sexual harassment today is just innocent flirting; it's been going on for years. People who claim that sexual harassment is a problem are simply not in touch with the reality in the new millennium.

5.5 It seems obvious that we have a problem in this country with violence. We have shootings in schools, violence on the streets, and a high rate of murder with handguns. Although we do have the right to bear arms, as outlined in the second amendment of the Constitution, we need to get a handle on the number of guns that are being used to commit crimes. We need to limit the amount of guns on the street. If we fail to do this, gun violence will continue to escalate. By taking a hard look at who can buy guns, we will be able to have some control over this problem. We simply can't continue to allow such easy access to guns.

Exercise 5.6

The Lottery Is a Tax on Stupid People
Agape Press, August 31, 2001
R. Cort Kirkwood
(Used with permission)

You knew it wouldn't be long before litigation muddied one of the big lottery payoffs. A group of office workers in Maine is looking to sue one of the winners of the recent $295 million Powerball game because her ticket, they argue, was purchased as part of an office pool. She says she bought her own.

Call it the apotheosis of greed in the 21st century. But also call the lottery what it is: A sucker's game, a social and fiscal scam on everyone.

The Numbers Game

Lotteries are immoral because the players really can't win, except by an astronomical stretch of fortune. As in most casino games, the odds are stacked against the player, who always loses even if he hits once in a while.

Indeed, the occasional hit is what keeps the loser coming back. If lottery players and casino gamblers could win consistently, neither lotteries nor casinos would be in business. If states paid out more than they earned, they'd go broke.

Of course the players themselves are partly to blame. Most don't understand statistics and probability, and therefore believe the more they play the better their chances. Some even believe it helps if they play the same number everyday.

Some day they'll hit a winner, but their premise is false. Consider a roulette wheel, which has 36 numbers: 34 black and red, and two green. Many players believe that by playing the No. 7 on every roll, eventually it must hit. Some roulette players even track the winning numbers to predict what's coming.

Well, 7 will hit, eventually, but only by pure luck. The chance of any given number hitting is the same with each roll of the ball: 38-to-1. If No. 11 comes up 1,000 times in a row, the chances of it coming again are 38-to-1.

Ditto for lotteries. You can play the same or a different number every day. You have the same chance of winning: practically none.

The Social Factor

On a social level, however, lotteries are bad as well. The state manipulates the impoverished playing on their urge to get rich quick, to fill its coffers for dubious public projects it cannot afford. The public schools addling our children are always a big beneficiary of lotteries, which is why voters approve these games at the ballot box.

Anyway, most lottery players are those who can least afford to lose money. If you don't think so, go into a 7-Eleven sometime and observe the professional lottery players on payday.

A typical scene is the halter-topped mother carting along a shirtless or shoeless toddler. With a six pack of Miller in one hand and a carton of Marlboros in the other, she rattles off the lottery combinations faster than a professional auctioneer. But she only earns minimum wage slinging hash at a greasy spoon.

Point is, lotteries prey upon lower-income people of lower intelligence to bloat the state's coffers. The irony of using the revenues for the public schools is this: The less intelligent are skinned to build schools that don't educate their children. This, of course, ensures a steady supply of lottery players.

An Immoral Tax

The lottery shows just how far the megastate and its elected officials will go to augment their power.

They prey upon those in lower income brackets who don't have the brains to know they're getting ripped off, or that riches do not lie in a painted ping-pong ball bobbing on a jet of air in a plastic cylinder.

Lotteries should be abolished. As a friend of mine once said, they're a tax on stupid people.

CHAPTER 6
Evidence

No argument is going to be believable without evidence. Can you imagine a prosecutor taking a case to court without any evidence? Can you imagine being persuaded to buy a used automobile without any evidence about its general condition or mileage? Could you accept a failing grade from a professor who doesn't provide any evidence for your failure? The most essential support material for any legitimate argument is its evidence.

But what exactly is evidence? Many people would suggest that evidence is facts. It's true that evidence is often factual, but not always, as we shall see. Do expert opinions count as evidence? Often people think numbers or statistics make good evidence. What about eyewitness accounts? Surely, the results of scientific research can be considered evidence.

Although there are many types of evidence, not all of it is credible. We need to be able to determine which evidence is believable and which is questionable. Only then can we start to evaluate the quality of the argument. Let's start by looking at the facts.

Fact versus Opinion

In the 1960's police drama, *Dragnet*, Sgt. Friday of the Los Angeles police department coined a phrase that we still use today. When he was interviewing a witness about a murder investigation, he would try to get the witness to leave out her ideas about the suspect or the crime and stick to what they actually knew or observed. "The facts, ma'am, just the facts."

We all know, on some level, what we mean by facts. Facts are pieces of information that are true. The height of the Eiffel Tower is a fact. It can be measured. Guidebooks list the height at 1,050 feet. For all practical purposes, we all agree on this fact. Somebody measured it. If we were to actually measure it, we might find that the figure of 1,050 feet is actually an approximation. In reality it may be 1,046.523 feet, but it IS a certain height. There is an absolute truth about its height.

Similarly, we would all agree that Mark McGwire hit seventy home runs in 1998, beating the previous record by nine home runs. He actually hit more, if we count exhibition games, but the factual record only counts home runs in regular season games. The press kept a close count, so we have no doubt that the number of seventy is accurate. We accept this as a fact.

What we accept as facts sometimes can be wrong. What if, on August 14, 1998, Mark McGwire hit a long ball that was very close to a home run, but was actually a foul ball? What if the umpire called it a home run by mistake? Then the fact would differ from what we perceive as the fact. The fact would be he hit sixty-nine home runs, but we would perceive the fact as seventy home runs.

Just because we perceive a fact as a fact, it may not be true. Nevertheless, we treat it as a fact and use it as a fact when we are reasoning. We have to do this. If we questioned every fact every time we used it, we would not be able to reach any conclusions. If we later discover that the fact is wrong, we can adjust our reasoning to accommodate this.

In an ideal world, we would have enough facts to use to figure out any problem, answer any question, or evaluate every argument. But we often don't have enough facts, so we must rely on another type of information: opinions. Opinions are not facts. They are people's ideas. They are not verifiable in the same way facts are. Often, opinions cannot be verified. Let's look at some examples.

If you were to plan a trip to Europe, you might read many guidebooks and decide to go to Italy. In planning your itinerary, you might decide to spend four days in Florence and two days in Rome. You might base this on your opinion that there is more you want to see in Florence than in Rome. That is clearly your opinion, not a fact. Different travelers would have different opinions about how much time to spend in a particular place. It is often a matter of personal preference. It is certainly not a fact.

When you shop, you must formulate opinions. Suppose you are looking for a new lamp for your living room. As you shop, you notice many lamps you like. You check the price of each lamp. This is factual information. Once you find a lamp you like, you must decide if the lamp is a good value. Is it worth the price? The price of the lamp is a fact. Whether or not it is a good value is an opinion.

How do we know whether or not to believe someone's opinion? Even though we would all agree that everyone has the right to an opinion, not all opinions are equal. Some opinions are based on careful consideration and factual information. Others are based on little other than personal bias. There may be no such thing as a good or bad opinion, but there is certainly an informed or uninformed opinion. When we hear or read an opinion, we need to try to figure out to what degree the opinion is an informed one. As a rule, we can put more stock in opinions that have been formulated as the result of careful consideration and research. We can value the opinions of people who have seriously investigated the issue. We must always exercise some degree of skepticism about any opinion, and we must try to evaluate the quality of any opinion.

We encounter both facts and opinions when we evaluate arguments. Our first task is to sort out the opinions from the facts. Let's consider the following example:

> Our community needs to spend more on education. Last year, we spent
> an average of 3,560 dollars for each student attending our public
> schools. Our students scored in the twenty-fifth percentile in English

and in the eighteenth percentile in math on the statewide tests last year. This is not acceptable. The average spending per student by communities throughout the state is $5,689. No wonder our students score lower!

Now let's list the facts this writer used in the argument:

Last year the community spent $3,560 per student on education.

The state average was $5,689.

The community's children scored in the twenty-fifth percentile in English and in the eighteenth percentile in math on last year's statewide tests.

These facts can be verified. We could look up the scores and check the school budgets. They are not arguable. They are facts.

Let's identify the opinions:

Our community needs to spend more on education.

It is not acceptable that our students score this low on the statewide tests.

Our students scored lower because we spent less on education.

Opinions are arguable. Not all people would agree with the author. Some might suggest that such low scores are acceptable and that we need not spend more on education. It is not always clear that the quality of education is directly related to the amount spent. These are not cut and dry like facts. They are less certain. So we need to evaluate them differently from facts. Opinions, by themselves, are not always believable. If they are supported by facts, they are more credible. In the above example, if the author cited a recent research study linking the quality of learning to the amount spent on education, we might find the opinion more believable. Opinions must be supported by evidence of some sort.

An argument is really an opinion. The conclusion of the argument is the author's opinion. The purpose of the argument is to present enough evidence to convince us to accept the author's opinion. The most common types of evidence offered in arguments include facts, statistics, expert opinion, personal observation, and research studies. We've already discussed facts; let's look at the other four types of evidence.

Statistics

Statistics are numbers. Numbers tend to make an argument look credible. When we read an argument that has lots of percentages, dollar figures, and other numbers, it often appears as though the author has done some research and really knows what he is talking about. This is not necessarily so. Numbers can be wrong. Even if the numbers are correct, they can be misleading. Numbers can be presented to show only part of the story. Before we can decide whether to believe any particular statistic and figure out if it is good evidence, we need to answer three questions:

1. Are the numbers likely to be accurate?
2. Do the numbers prove what the author claims they prove?
3. Have any important numbers been left out?

Let's take each of these questions separately. First, **are the numbers likely to be accurate?** Our first task in evaluating statistics is to determine whether the numbers are likely to be correct. We need to find information about where the author got these figures. Were they simply inserted into the argument without explaining where they came from? This may be fine if the numbers are commonly known or are easily accessible. To use our previous example, if an author claims the Eiffel Tower is 1,050 feet tall, and does not list a source, then this is not a serious problem. This is a fact that easily can be checked, and from our experience it sounds reasonable. Similarly, if an arguer claimed that 40 million Americans are presently enrolled in the Medicare program without explaining where the information came from, it would not be a serious problem with the argument because this information could be verified, and it sounds reasonable.

If the numbers are not commonly known, are not easy to check, or sound unreasonable, then the source should be revealed. For example, if an author claimed that one third of the children in the United States were severely beaten as children and did not explain where those figures came from, we should be skeptical. That sounds like a high number, and we would not be able to verify it easily.

Sometimes, even if the source is revealed, we need to be careful before believing the statistics. If the source is biased or has something to gain from the argument, we should be especially skeptical. As an example, if the U.S. Used Car Dealers Association (USUCDA) published figures indicating that their research showed ninety-five percent of used car purchasers in a given year were satisfied with their purchases, we would have to be skeptical. Not only does it appear to be high, but it might have been influenced by the way the USUCDA collected the data. After all, they certainly had a stake in its outcome.

Even if we can assure ourselves that the numbers themselves are correct, we need to ask, **do the numbers prove what the author claims they prove?** Often, writers will manipulate statistical data to suggest that their conclusion is true, when, in fact, the statistics may not actually bear that out. Consider the following argument:

Try our new HOMETOWN HMO. We have been in business for over three years, and during that time period, only two percent of our patients

have filed formal complaints with our services. With a ninety-eight
percent patient satisfaction rate, we should be your HMO.

Just because only two percent of the patients formally complained, we cannot be sure
that the remaining ninety-eight percent were satisfied. What about informal
complaints? What about those who were dissatisfied but felt as though it would do no
good to complain? In actuality, a two percent formal complaint rate may be quite
high. Let's look at another example:

> Although they make up only two percent of the drivers, sixteen and
> seventeen-year-olds are involved in nineteen percent of the crashes.
> That indicates that they are unsafe drivers. Also, sixty-three percent of
> the accidents teenagers get into are one-car accidents, usually caused
> by poor judgment.

The author is using statistics to try to prove that teens are unsafe drivers. Assuming
the statistics are accurate, this does not necessarily prove what the author claims. The
fact that sixteen-seventeen-year-olds are "involved in" nineteen percent of the crashes
does not prove that they were responsible for these accidents. Similarly, how do we
know that one-car crashes necessarily indicate poor judgment? And as far as the
sixty-three percent goes, how does that compare to the percentage of all crashes, at
all age groups, which involve only one car. You easily can see that these statistics,
although they sound good, do not necessarily prove what the author suggests.

When evaluating an argument that uses statistics, we need to evaluate carefully what
the statistics represent. We need to consider if the point the author is making is
actually supported by the numbers provided. Think of what kind of numbers would
actually prove what the author is trying to prove, and compare this with the actual
numbers provided. To use the above example, if we really wanted to know if teens
were unsafe drivers, we would need to compare the accident rates of teen drivers with
those of older drivers. The author did not do this.

Finally, we need to ask, **have any important numbers been left out?** People who want
to deceive with statistics will only show the numbers that seem to support their
position. By omitting numbers that might weaken their case, they are intentionally
misleading. Look at the following:

> Cancer research in this country clearly favors women. It is true that
> roughly one in ten women will get breast cancer at some time in their
> lives, and that one in ten men will get prostate cancer. Yet, over four
> times the money is spent on researching cures for breast cancer than
> cures for prostate cancer. What's going on?

Assuming these figures are accurate, they still don't tell the whole story. This
argument refers to the incidence of both of these types of cancer, but it does not
address the death rates of each type. It also does not reveal the ages of the cancer

victims. Prostate cancer is most likely to strike elderly men who will not die of the cancer. Breast cancer, on the other hand, kills many younger women. These additional statistics might present a different picture that would not support the author's conclusion that research discriminates against men.

Another type of statistical omission is to include percentages but not raw numbers. This can be very misleading, as the following example illustrates:

> Students from our home state are clearly superior in terms of academic preparation than those from other states. At our local community college, the average GPA for in-state students last year was 2.65, with a graduation rate of eighty-two percent. For out-of-state students last year, the average GPA was 1.53 with a graduation rate of only fifty percent. Our secondary schools must be doing an excellent job.

What's been omitted from this argument is the total number of students in each category. Most community colleges have very few out-of-state students. If the number of in-state students was 850, and the number of out-of-state students was two, then the percentages would mean little. If one of the out-of-state students flunked out, that would represent a fifty percent failure rate, but it would be unreasonable to apply that percentage to all out-of-state students. So if you are examining percentages, consider the raw numbers as well.

Although statistics can add relevant and meaningful data to an argument, we have to be careful and examine the use of statistics to see if they merit our belief. Remain skeptical.

Expert Opinion

Experts are everywhere. We cannot turn on the television without being bombarded by experts telling us how to raise our children, how to keep from aging, or what to do to prepare for our retirement. When we are in a crisis, we turn to experts: physicians for medical assistance, lawyers for legal advice, and computer consultants for help when our computers crash. This makes sense. After all, these people have presumably learned a tremendous amount about their area of expertise. They have studied, read, talked with other experts, and their advice is widely sought.

Experts' opinions are often cited as evidence in arguments. Their advice is solicited, and their opinion is often put forth as truth. But is all this expert opinion correct? Of course not! Experts will freely admit that they often make educated guesses with limited facts. They often disagree with one another, so they cannot all be right. Our job is to try to figure out what to believe and what to take with a grain of salt. When we encounter expert opinion, we have to examine it closely before we can make a determination. First of all, as we have already discussed, we should always be skeptical. Never accept the opinion of any expert as gospel; always remember that they are fallible. Beyond that, you need to consider several questions when considering the testimony of an expert:

1. How is this person qualified to offer an expert opinion on this subject?

2. Who is paying this person to offer an opinion?

3. Does this person reveal the evidence and reasoning behind her position?

4. To what degree do other experts agree with this person?

Let's take each of these questions in turn. **How is this person qualified to offer an expert opinion on this subject?** This is an important consideration because there are many so-called experts who routinely offer advice well beyond their area of expertise. Just because a person has gone to law school does not qualify him as an expert in all areas of law. What area of law has he practiced? How many similar cases has he litigated? Similarly, university professors are usually uniquely qualified in one or two narrow areas of scholarly research. Beyond those areas, their expertise is often less impressive. The amount of knowledge has grown so much in such a short period of time that we cannot expect anyone to be an expert in more than a relatively narrow area.

So when you are confronted with the opinion of experts, try to figure out what qualifies them to be considered as experts in this area. If you can't get much information about this, you need to accept their opinion with a considerable degree of skepticism.

One final note about this: increasingly, journalists are moving into the area of making predictions and offering opinions on a variety of topics. Gone are the days when the media simply reported the facts and let the viewers or readers decide for themselves. Today, as the competitive market drives the news organizations, journalists are putting themselves forward as experts in their own right. We need to keep in mind that they have little to no expertise in the areas on which they are reporting, and they are often wrong.

Another important consideration to keep in mind when evaluating expert opinion is the issue of conflict of interest. **Who is paying this person to offer an opinion?** Experts do not work for free. Their opinions are often worth a considerable amount of money to others who may stand to gain from their persuasiveness. A good example of this is the use of expert opinions in criminal trials. Criminal defense attorneys will pay expert witnesses to offer their testimony to support their client's position. Prosecutors will hire other experts to offer testimony that contradicts the testimony of the defense witnesses. Some individuals earn a considerable living by appearing as expert witnesses, being paid by whomever needs their testimony. In this example, truth is often the first casualty. If individuals are paid to offer conflicting testimony, it becomes very difficult to trust the information on either side.

As a general rule of thumb, if an expert is being paid by an individual or an organization that has a financial or other stake in the testimony, we should be extremely skeptical of his testimony. After all, scientific experts who work for the tobacco companies have argued for years that there is no conclusive evidence that smoking is dangerous for one's health. Experts work for all major corporations, organizations, and special interest groups, and it's not surprising that their opinions tend to support the economic and political interests of their employers.

Sometimes, expert opinions are put forward without any explanation, so it's important to check to see if the expert has **revealed the evidence supporting her position.** Read or listen to the testimony of an expert carefully. Do they provide evidence to support their position? How much information do they provide? Do they clearly explain their reasoning behind their opinion? Often, you will be able to tell a good deal about the quality of an expert opinion by listening to the details. If there are few or no details, be skeptical. It could be that they have not presented the details because of lack of space or lack of time. But before you accept the expert opinion, get the details.

A good example of this would be going to the doctor. When we receive a diagnosis from a physician, especially if it concerns a serious condition, we should be ready to discuss how she reached her diagnosis. How certain is it? Are there any other possible diagnoses which that fit with the same data? What is the possibility she might be wrong?

Finally, we must determine the **degree to which other experts agree on this position.** No human, no matter how intelligent or how conscientious, is correct all the time. That's why it's important that we don't accept a single opinion as the truth. If the opinion is supported by a large number of other experts, it may be more likely that the opinion is a valid one. This is not always true, of course. Sometimes, new ideas that have merit are dismissed by other experts simply because they don't fit with previous thinking. But in general, expert opinions, which are supported by others independently, tend to be more valid than those which are not.

So expert opinion is certainly a valid type of evidence. But, like any other type of evidence, it must be examined closely.

Personal Observation

Another common type of evidence is personal testimony derived from experience or observation. This type of evidence has traditionally been highly valued because it comes from someone who has had personal experience with the issue at hand. Eyewitness accounts are usually compelling and often dramatic. In court, witnesses who have actually viewed a crime taking place are used whenever possible.

Although personal observation or experience can be useful, we need to exercise some caution when evaluating it as evidence. We must remember that, even though it is based on someone's personal experience, it is not always reliable. Eyewitness accounts of crimes, for example, may differ substantially from one another. Two people watching an event will often view it differently. Police work routinely involves debriefing witnesses who think they saw an event one way that conflicts with the way other witnesses saw the same event. Different people tend to focus on different aspects of their experience. Stress or other emotional interference can get in the way of getting an accurate picture of what went on. One's ability to recall accurately is fallible too. People tend to report an event in a way that casts them in the most favorable light. For many reasons, personal observation cannot just be accepted as fact.

Another problem with evidence that is based exclusively on the observation or experience of one individual is that it is very limited. We refer to this type of evidence as **anecdotal**, meaning that it is just an example, and not necessarily a representative one. Let's look at a common example. Suppose you were in the market for a vehicle. You have been looking at a particular brand, let's say a Saturn. You've looked at a number of Saturns and you are leaning toward buying one. You are speaking to a close friend about this, and he tells you," Whatever you do, don't buy a Saturn! My father-in-law bought one last year, and he sure regrets it now. He's had nothing but trouble with that car. In fact the engine died after 52,000 miles!" Now this may seem to be a legitimate piece of evidence and may even dissuade you from buying a Saturn. But what is the problem with this evidence? It's too limited. The fact that one Saturn was a lemon means nothing. You don't know how typical this is of these vehicles. In fact, you don't even know how well, or how poorly, this vehicle was maintained.

This is probably the primary problem with personal experience as evidence. No matter how reliable it is, it is anecdotal and rarely proves anything. Many times, in an argument, an author will try to prove a point by using a specific case or a personal example. In an argument making a case for tightening up on welfare fraud, for example, the author might cite a case of a woman in Oklahoma who bilked the welfare system for thousands of dollars and drove a fancy car and could afford to take exotic vacations. Even if this example is true, how typical is it? Of all the people collecting welfare benefits, how many of them bilk the system? This example might be effective, because it appeals to the reader's emotions, but it is not good evidence.

The final problem with evidence that relies on personal experience is that it can easily be biased. The person upon whose observation or experience the evidence is based might have some emotional or financial stake in the issue that could affect his judgment. Let's use the example of an argument to increase the school budget. Perhaps the writer of such an argument would use the testimony of one of the teachers in the school system to help make the case that the school district needs more money. The teacher could, of course, provide an inside view of the problem and may be able to share information that could be considered important in deciding whether to allot more money to the schools. However, we need to keep in mind that the teacher might very well benefit personally from such a decision. He might get an increase in his salary. His job may become more secure. No matter how well intentioned he may be, his opinion is clearly biased.

So how should we view personal observation and experience as evidence in an argument? Obviously it is important and may provide some useful information for us.

But this type of evidence, by its very nature, is limited. It should never be accepted by itself. This type of evidence always needs to be substantiated by other types of evidence.

Research Studies

Perhaps the most compelling of all types of evidence is the scientific research study. This type of research is conducted regularly and is widely reported by the media. Scarcely a day goes by without some new report of some food which we all thought was safe being linked to some type of terrible disease. Or conversely, we may hear reports that certain types of foods or vitamins may provide protection against cancer or heart disease. We read about research completed to measure the effect of TV violence on juvenile delinquency. Research is conducted on virtually every aspect of our lives. The results of such studies, because they are conducted under the guise of science, are regularly used as scientific "proof." Because we have so much faith in, and often little understanding of, the limits and methodologies of these studies, we tend to accept the results as true. This is dangerous. Just like other types of evidence, research studies vary in quality, and we need to examine a number of factors carefully before deciding to accept these results as valid. We need to be able to know who did the study, why it was done, and how it was done. The problem is, we often do not have access to all this information. Such research often is reported in the media in a very abbreviated form, making it difficult or impossible to get the information we need. But if the research is valid, this information is generally available in the original publication that published the study. We can obtain this original article either through the library or over the Internet.

The first question we have to ask when evaluating a research study is, **Who conducted the study?** Was the study designed and carried out by a reputable research institution or organization? Did the researchers have any bias or point of view we can detect?

Who published the study? Is it a serious, research-oriented publication?

Who financed the study? Does this organization have any financial stake in the results? A study on the health benefits of oat bran, for example, financed by Quaker Oats, could be biased.

Another important factor to consider is, **Has the study been replicated?** Is this the only study that achieved these results, or have others done it as well? As a general rule, the more often a study has been replicated, the more likely the results are accurate. If this is the only study of its type that has been done, then we should wait for more follow-up studies before putting too much stock in this result. A famous example of this occurred in the 1980's when two U.S. scientists claimed to have achieved cold fusion in the laboratory. Cold fusion, if it can be achieved, would provide a source of low cost, clean energy for the future, much safer that nuclear fission. Unfortunately, when other scientists tried to replicate their results, they were unsuccessful. What the media heralded as an energy breakthrough still remains only a possibility.

The most important information about a research study involves its **methodology, or the procedure that was used to conduct the study.** And the first item to consider about the method is the **sample** used. The sample refers to the experimental group. It could be the people who took an experimental drug. It could be a group of individuals who were asked survey questions. It even could be a group of statistical data which was evaluated. But most research studies involve some sort of sample which is studied in some way. The results of the study are then applied in a more general way to the broader population. For example, if a new drug proves to be effective in a small group of cancer patients, it may well prove helpful to many patients who have certain types of cancer.

The first question we need to address is the **size of the sample.** Generally speaking, the larger the sample, the more likely we are to get accurate results that would match the general population. Consider this example. If we wanted to know whether or not aspirin was effective in relieving headaches, we might give it to two people and see if they report any relief. This, of course, wouldn't prove much. Whatever we discovered would only be true for these two people, and it wouldn't necessarily apply to everyone. If, on the other hand, we tried this with 1,000 people, we'd likely get a more reliable result.

The size of the sample, however, is not the only factor. **Random samples** are always preferable to non-random ones. A random sample means that everyone has an equal chance of being selected. To use the example of our headache study, if we asked for 1,000 volunteers to participate in the study, we might get people who have a lot of trouble with headaches who are looking forward to getting some relief. This might affect the results, because perhaps these people have the types of headaches that are less treatable by aspirin alone. So such a study that used volunteer participants might show a different result than if 1,000 people were selected at random out of a phone book, many of whom only had occasional headaches. It is possible that aspirin might be much more effective in relieving occasional headaches than chronic severe headaches. So the random sample would give us more reliable information about the effect of aspirin on headaches among the general population.

Another factor that we need to consider about the sample is its **breadth or diversity.** In general, the more diverse the sample, the more reliable the result. Let's use the headache study again, as an example. Suppose the sample included just women, or just African Americans, or just people from the Midwest, or just professional people.

There may be factors within these groups that could affect the incidence of headaches or the effectiveness of aspirin. To get a more generalizable study, we would need a more diverse group. In fact, using a random sample often creates a diverse sample as well.

Another important consideration is the **design of the study.** How was the study conducted? We must examine this closely to look for possible sources of error. For example, in the headache study, how will the effectiveness of aspirin be measured? Will the participants simply tell the researchers how often they had headaches and how often they took aspirin, and how effective it was? Or will the subjects go to the clinic when they are suffering from a headache to get the aspirin? Will they live in a laboratory setting or will they live at home and conduct their regular activities? Will they refrain from taking any other drugs while they are taking the aspirin so the researchers can more effectively measure the effect of the aspirin? Will there be a control group that takes a placebo, or a sugar pill, so the headache relief experienced by those who took aspirin can be compared to the headache relief by those who took the placebo? As we can see, there are many factors to consider, any one of which could affect the result of the study.

Here are some factors that can enhance the result of a research study:

The use of a control group: A control group is a group that is treated in exactly the same way as the experimental group except that it is not exposed to the experimental procedure. For example, if a drug company wants to measure how effective a drug is, it will administer the drug to some patients and a placebo to the others. Sometimes, people report an effect because they are expecting an effect. The use of the placebo will indicate whether the effect on the group receiving the drug differs significantly from the group receiving the placebo.

The ability to isolate what is being measured: This is a very difficult problem. It is important, when designing a study, that the variable being researched is isolated from other possible variables that could affect the result. For example, if research is being conducted to determine if exercise improves health, and the researchers measure how much exercise the subjects do and then assess their overall health, how do they know that the effect on the subjects' health is from the exercise alone. Wouldn't people who exercise also have other healthy habits like eating well and refraining from smoking? It is often impossible to completely isolate the variable, but the better studies make every effort to do so by taking other factors into account. This is a fundamental problem with clinical studies of all sorts. The human body is very complex and the effect of a particular substance on the body is not measured easily because of the possible interaction of other variables of which the researchers may not be aware. Therefore, most clinical research studies must be viewed with caution. This is another reason why replication (getting similar results in other studies) is so important.

Methods to eliminate possible bias of the researchers: Competent researchers make every effort to eliminate their own possible bias. If a researcher is looking for a particular result, she may tend to filter out results that don't match her preconceived result. This can be a big problem especially when continued funding may be dependent upon making progress in research. Therefore, effective research employs some method to eliminate this researcher bias. The most common type is the double blind study, where neither the researcher nor the subject knows whether the subject is in the experimental group or the control group. In the headache study, a double blind procedure would prevent the researcher and the patient from knowing whether the patient was taking an aspirin or a placebo until the end of the experiment.

The use of a longitudinal study: Longitudinal studies are those that are conducted over a period of time. Some of these studies, like the now-famous Framingham Heart Study, are conducted over many years. Longitudinal studies are generally the most effective because they measure effects over time and allow comparisons that could not otherwise be made. A cross-sectional study, in contrast, is one that simply takes a snapshot of a population at a given point in time. This may be useful, but is generally not as accurate as a longitudinal study. Of course longitudinal studies take a considerable period of time and are usually expensive.

The use of a natural environment: Some studies are conducted in a laboratory, while others allow the subjects to remain in a natural environment. The advantage of using a laboratory-based experiment is that it allows the researchers to control the variables more reliably. For example, if the subjects lived in a lab for 30 days, and the diet was completely controlled, then the results might be more reliable. With human subjects, however, laboratory-based experiments of any length are difficult to set up because it is difficult to recruit subjects. Many animal experiments, however, are conducted in laboratory environments. These types of experiments raise ethical questions because of the effects on the experimental subjects. For this reason, most clinical studies on humans are conducted while the subject remains in a normal living environment. This is desirable because subjects in an experimental setting often do not react the way they would in a natural environment. But, as we've already noted, it does become difficult to control the variable being measured.

The independent collection of data rather than relying on self reporting: One common problem with collecting data is the reliability of the data. This is particularly true when the researchers are relying on self-reported data from the subjects. For example, if you ask subjects to take two aspirin every time they get a headache, and record when they do this, you have no way of knowing whether or not they actually did what they reported. This is a particular problem when subjects are asked to report undesirable behavior. If asked how often they drink alcohol, for example, most subjects tend to underreport this. Therefore, it is usually more reliable when the data collected is collected independently. For example, a study that is measuring a drug designed to lower the blood cholesterol levels can rely on laboratory-evaluated blood samples. This data is going to be more reliable that a study that relies on subjects to self-report on the incidence of headaches. Often, researchers have no choice but to rely on self-reported data. But such research needs to be assessed with more skepticism.

One common type of research methodology involves the use of **surveys or questionnaires** to gather information directly from people. It may be in the form of a poll done during a political campaign. It may be a questionnaire about a product you receive in the mail. It may be part of a medical study researching the side effects of medication, asking patients to respond to written questions about how they feel and any symptoms they are experiencing. Any type of data collection that involves asking people questions can be problematic.

The first problem surveyors face is determining the truthfulness of the responses. People may tend to exaggerate or shade the truth when they give a response to a surveyor. As we discussed earlier, this is particularly true when they are asked about behavior that might be perceived as undesirable. Respondents don't want to appear in a bad light, so they may not be entirely truthful. For this reason, it's important to understand exactly how the survey was conducted. A simple questionnaire a person receives in the mail and returns without their name on it might elicit more reliable information than the same questions asked in a face to face setting, for example. The problem is getting people to return questionnaires by mail. It's important to keep in mind that people may not be entirely truthful in surveys.

Perhaps the greatest problem with survey methodology is the use of **leading or ambiguous questions.** People's response to survey questions will vary considerably depending on how the question is worded. As an example, let's examine several questions that could be worded to elicit a response about how well the mayor is doing in terms of obtaining funding for the local schools. Consider each of the following questions:

> 1. How satisfied are you that the mayor's *reduced budget* this year will be able to meet the increasing needs of our schools, *our most important investment?*

> 2. How well do you think the mayor is doing in keeping costs down in the face of *increasing demands* by the school board to *significantly boost* the school budget?

> 3. How well do you think the mayor is doing in addressing the needs of the schools?

Each of these questions might tend to elicit a different response. Each of the first two questions use language, indicated in Italics, which indicates a possible bias. The first question tends to expect a negative response, while the second question seems to expect a positive one. The third question maintains a more neutral tone. Research surveys can be used to create data that the researcher is looking for if the questions are worded in a biased way. Political candidates, corporations, and special interest groups frequently use these types of surveys, not to arrive at the truth, but to manipulate the truth to serve their own needs. For this reason, whenever we see research that utilizes the results of surveys, we should remain especially skeptical and try to view copies of the actual questions used.

Research studies are a valid form of research, which often provide necessary and useful information. But many such studies are seriously flawed which, by themselves, prove little. Many people are skeptical about all research, which is unfortunate because some research is extremely valuable. We need to become good consumers of research and evaluate any study before we are willing to accept its results as the truth.

When evaluating arguments, we need to examine all the evidence the author presents. By looking under the surface and probing, we can go far in determining if the evidence is reliable and provides good enough reasoning to accept the conclusion.

Exercise 6.1

Classify each of the following as a fact or an opinion.

a. Green tea is good for the heart.

b. Cigarette smoke contains nicotine.

c. Peter Wood is a wealthy man.

d. Stephen King is a published author.

e. Fifty-five percent of marriages eventually end in divorce.

f. Poverty is a serious problem for this country.

g. Everyone who wants to get a good job should go to college.

h. Critical thinking is a useful skill.

i. Most college students in 1999 were women.

j. People who smoke cigarettes run a greater risk of getting lung cancer than do non-smokers.

k. People who smoke are careless about their health.

l. It is wrong to abuse young children.

In the following exercises, (1) DIAGRAM the arguments (2) IDENTIFY and EXPLAIN any ambiguous words or phrases, and (3) EVALUATE the quality of the evidence:

6.2 Many young families rely on daycare centers to provide care for their children while they work. Although many young moms would rather stay at home with their children than work outside the home, that is not always possible. Many have always assumed that having a mother at home with the children is better for the children's development, but this is not true. According to Dr. Richard Benjamin, a Chicago pediatrician, "Children need regular social interaction with other children. Daycare centers can provide this." Also, in a recent study completed of freshmen at Harvard University, the grade point averages of those students who were, as children, in day-care four or more days a week was not significantly different from those students who had never attended daycare. In fact, ask most adults who were in daycare centers as children; they will hardly ever cite it as a problem in their later life.

6.3 Try new Ginkosyne available at GNC. This dietary supplement is now available to everyone. For centuries, the ancient Chinese used an ingredient similar to that in Ginkosyne to maintain health and preserve energy. Clinical studies completed within the last year demonstrate that people who took Ginkosyne every day had 35% more energy than those who did not. Marge Peterson from Owensburg, Ohio writes, "Ginkosyne has made a big difference in my life. I was suffering from low energy, insomnia, and a general feeling of hopelessness. Since taking Ginkosyne every day, I feel great. Thank you Ginkosyne!" Dr. Harry Schweickhardt, M.D., a former Food and Drug Administration physician, states, "Ginkosyne is perfectly safe. You can use it as directed without any side effects."

6.4 Large doses of Vitamin C not only may *not* help, they may cause medical problems, according to a new study published in the journal *Nature*. Joseph Lunec, of the University of Leicester University in England gave healthy volunteers 500 milligrams of vitamin C every day for six weeks. Before the treatment, and again during the treatment, researchers measured oxidation damage to the volunteer's cells. The cells showed increased oxidation damage while they were taking the high doses of Vitamin C. Five hundred milligrams is eight times the recommended daily dose. At higher doses, Lunec suggested, the negative effects may be even more pronounced.

6.5 Well, the evidence is in. The new computer programs designed to teach students to write are at least as effective as teaching students to write the more traditional way, with a teacher. According to a study completed recently at Calhoun College, students who used the computers to study writing learned slightly more effectively than students in traditional classes. The entering freshmen were placed in either a traditional writing class or in a computerized writing lab. The students in the traditional class received standard instruction. The students in the computer class worked independently with the WRITERIGHT software. At the end of the study, eighty-six percent of the students in the computer classes believed they had improved their writing "significantly" compared to seventy-eight percent of the students enrolled in the traditional classes. Additionally, ninety percent of the computer class students found learning to write "easy" compared to only twenty-three percent of the traditional students. All the students from both classes took the Brigham Grammar and Spelling assessment tool at the end of the course, and there was virtually no difference in the scores between the two groups.

Exercise 6.6

The Lost Art of Writing
Lewiston (Maine) Sun Journal: June 8, 2003
Silvio Laccetti and Scott Molski
(Used with permission)

Millions of America's high school and college students cannot write well. The problem is worsening, according to the recent report of the National Commission on Writing in America's Schools and Colleges. Poor writing among our students is not only an educational problem; it has cultural and economic ramifications as well. Good writing has become a lost art.

What is the importance of writing? Well, for starters, the development of writing was a vital element in creating civilized life. Writing expanded communication and gave direction to public and economic life. Good writing enables memory of the individual and the culture since it provides records and models of events. Superior writing inspires the imagination taking humanity to ever-higher potential.

Why, then, can't Johnny and Jane write well? According to a recent press release from the commission, there are several key factors that greatly hinder the abilities of America's students. First, there is a lack of writing assignments in the schools. Most fourth-grade students spend fewer than three hours writing during their 35 hours per week in the classroom.

Approximately 66 percent of high school seniors do not write a three-page paper as often as once a month for English class. About 75 percent never receive any writing assignment in history or social studies.

Additionally, few high-school seniors ever write the mysterious senior research paper, because teachers do not have the time to grade such projects. Furthermore, almost no students pursue writing out of school.

Besides the general writing problem, there is a greater deficiency of writing skills in specific sectors, especially among engineering and science students. For decades, the major complaint from the business world upon hiring technical graduates has been their poor writing skills. University administrators respond by stating that their students take courses in writing and have numerous writing labs, and that more cannot be done without sacrificing the core classes. However, sacrificing strong writing skills comes at a very high price.

According to Impact Information, a firm that specializes in improving writing and communication skills, highly skilled and highly paid workers can spend as much as 85 percent of their time writing. Then, once these technical workers under perform in their writing, higher-paid executives need to review and revise documents. Thus, the corporations spend a significant amount of money not on their core competencies but on creating readable documents.

Technology is also partly to blame for the poor writing skills of American students. In any college dorm there is a computer, television and various other interactive, content-driven gizmos.

The computer is the worst offender: College and high school students sit at their machines e-mailing and instant messaging without proofreading, revising or giving much thought to what they have written. The errors then continue to be circulated and repeated by others until finally everyone on the Internet has become illiterate, replacing proper English with Internet slang.

Unfortunately for these students, their bosses will not be "LOL" when they read a report that lacks proper punctuation and grammar, has numerous misspellings, various made-up words, and silly acronyms.

Further problems occur with television and its advertising. Television deprives students of reading time. Without exposure to great literature, or reading for its own sake, students have no idea what a literate phrase is supposed to look like. However, they are able to quote verbatim from last week's episode of "Friends"!

Advertising is also an issue; companies like to make up words. For example, many man-hours were devoted to making sure that the name "Exxon" had no meaning in any language. "Verizon" is also a made-up word, created from two real words. Many other meaningless and misspelled words are becoming household names through advertising.

Most important, America can fall behind in the global economy because of poor writing skills. Reading and writing often, and writing well, inspire creativity, encourages abstract thought, and explain or document innovation. If Americans lose these traits, they will be hobbled in the increasingly competitive global marketplace.

What now to do about this lack of writing ability among American students? Heeding complaints of teachers and educational associations is a good start. The SAT will soon include a new section of writing, with the hope that this measure will force teachers to emphasize writing. However, testing is not the only answer.

The lifestyles and attitudes of Americans must change. People need to return to reading books instead of watching television. Teachers need to move away from multiple-choice tests and have students write more essays.

Students must recognize the need to write well and seek to acquire the proper skills. They must actively practice good writing on their own, whether it be electronic, hard copy, for school or for pleasure.

The education, corporate and political establishments must recognize the value of a literate culture and reward those who actively participate in it.

America needs leaders who can effectively express their ideas. America needs students who are masters of the lost art of writing.

CHAPTER 7
Assumptions: The Unstated Reasoning

What Is an Assumption?

In critical thinking, as we have seen in previous chapters, we must always be careful to make certain that we have enough information to make good decisions. Before we decide to buy a car, for example, we collect as much evidence on that automobile as we can. We might read the review in *Consumer Reports* to see how the repair record on the model we are considering stacks up against other models. We might take the car to a mechanic for an expert opinion. We collect as much information as we can ourselves by looking at the car carefully for evidence of problems. Collecting evidence is an essential part of making an intelligent decision.

There is some information that we do not actively seek, however. We do not, for example, check inside the gas tank to make sure someone has not put foreign material into it. We do not remove the fuel pump and have someone check it for factory defects. In most cases, we do not check to see if the odometer has been tampered with. We take it for granted that these problems, and many others, are not present. It would be impractical to check for these things because they are unlikely to have occurred. We assume that they have not.

An assumption is a belief or fact that we accept as true without examining it closely. When we make an assumption, we do not question or test it; we use it as if it were true. Sometimes assumptions are reasonable; sometimes they are unreasonable. However, we could not think or make decisions unless we made some assumptions.

Think about how many such assumptions we make during an average day. We assume that we will not die during the night when we plan for the next day. We assume the other drivers will obey the rules of the road when we drive. We assume our instructor will be there when we show up for class. We assume the television station is still broadcasting when we turn on the TV. We assume no one has poisoned our food when we eat. The number of assumptions we make in a day is innumerable. It is not difficult to make assumptions because we usually don't think about them. Sometimes we are wrong, but the vast majority of the time we are correct.

Types of Assumptions

Most of the time, our assumptions are **unconscious**; that is, we make them without knowing we are making them. Each of the examples in the previous paragraph is an unconscious assumption. Although unconscious assumptions are a necessary part of our everyday thinking, they can be dangerous when they are incorrect. If two electricians are working on a circuit, and each assumes the other turned off the power to the circuit, then the results could be tragic. A mother who leaves her sleeping child at home alone for a few minutes may assume he will not waken. A driver assumes, as she comes to the top of a hill, that any oncoming vehicle will be in its own lane. In each of these cases, assumptions were made without considering whether they were true or not. The person making the assumption probably did not really think about the fact that she was assuming anything.

Sometimes we make **conscious** assumptions. We may not know whether they are true, but they help us make decisions. Let's say we own a small mom and pop convenience store, and we want to expand to allow more space for our returnable bottles. In order to decide how large to make the addition, we must make an **assumption** about the amount of business we will likely get. We understand that we cannot know, for sure, but we must make a conscious, or working, assumption so we can plan the project. To use another example, let's consider a couple planning for their retirement. They want to decide how to invest their money now so they have enough money on which to retire. In order to plan their investment, they must make a number of conscious assumptions. They may assume that they will earn a certain interest rate on their money over the years. They may assume that the pension they are contributing toward will pay at the same rate it is paying retirees now. They may also assume that inflation will continue to grow at a specific rate each year. Their assumptions may or may not be correct, but if they made no assumptions, they would not be able to plan for their financial future.

Assumptions can also be classified as **warranted** or **unwarranted**. Warranted assumptions are those that are reasonable. It is reasonable to assume that when we show up for class, the instructor will be there. Of course, our assumption may be incorrect. The instructor might be sick or have car trouble and be unable to attend class. However, our assumption was warranted. Our past experience has told us that instructors usually show up for class and that this instructor is usually reliable. A warranted assumption is one that is based on reasonable beliefs and is supported by the preponderance of evidence available.

An unwarranted assumption, obviously, is one which is unreasonable. If a student receives an A on the first two graded assignments in a course, he may be tempted to assume that the course will be easy and that he will easily be able to get an A in the course. This is an unwarranted assumption because it is reasonably likely that the course will become more difficult as the semester proceeds. Many older students starting college after a long absence from school may make the unwarranted assumption that they will be unable to do the work because they are out of practice. In fact, older students often make the best students because they have the motivation and determination to do thorough work. Another common unwarranted assumption is the "I thought you were going to do it!" assumption. How many times have we assumed our spouse, a coworker, or someone else was going to complete a task while they were assuming the same about us? The inevitable result: the job remains undone.

Identifying and Evaluating Assumptions in Arguments

Just as we make assumptions in our everyday lives, we also make assumptions when we construct arguments. We do not explicitly state every idea that is essential for our reasoning. We take certain ideas for granted when we argue for a conclusion.

When we are examining an argument to determine the quality of its reasoning, we need to be able to identify and examine any unstated (implicit) assumptions the author is making before we can thoroughly evaluate the reasoning. In fact, for every reason in an argument, there is an assumption which connects that reason to the conclusion. It may be an obvious assumption, but this is not always the case.

For example, let's examine the following simple argument:

Reason: I have won the state lottery.

Conclusion: Now I can quit my job.

This may be a sound argument, but it is based on one very important assumption: *the money from the lottery will make up for my salary.* So, if we were to accept this argument as sound, we would have to identify that assumption and then evaluate it to see if it were likely to be true. If it were not, then we would have to conclude that the argument was flawed.

Let's examine some other simple arguments:

Reason: The unemployment rate was higher than expected last month.

Conclusion: The economy is still weak.

Assumption: *The unemployment rate is a reasonable indicator of the health of the economy.*

Many economists would disagree with the assumption in this case, arguing that the unemployment rate is the last indicator to decline when an economy is emerging from a recession. If we accept this reasoning, then the conclusion is unreasonable.

Reason: The jury has taken five full days to deliberate, and they still have not reached a verdict.

Conclusion: The judge may have to declare a mistrial.

Assumption: *The reason the jury is taking so long to reach a decision is that the jury is divided.*

This assumption makes the conclusion reasonable because unless a jury is unanimous in its verdict, it is considered a hung jury which usually results in a mistrial. Of course, it is possible that the jury is not divided but is just taking a lot of time to sort through the evidence. If this is true, then the assumption is incorrect and the conclusion is not reasonable.

Reason: The Red Sox have won eight of the first ten games of the season.

Conclusion: They will win the American League East pennant.

Assumption: *They will continue to win games at a similar rate.*

As any baseball fan knows, the assumption, however appealing, is unwarranted. With 162 games, an eighty percent winning average is unlikely for any team.

Reason: This winter has been 20% colder than normal.

Conclusion: My heating bill will be higher than normal.

Assumption: *My heating bill goes up as the temperature goes down.*

This assumption is reasonable unless insulation has been added to the home or the heating system has been modified to make it more efficient. Therefore, the conclusion is most likely reasonable.

Reason: I have been late to work sixteen times during the last six months.

Conclusion: I will be fired.

Assumption: *My employer values punctuality and considers excessive lateness a sufficient reason for termination.*

It is very possible that such tardiness would be considered unacceptable by an employer. Although, if the employer considered other aspects of the employee's job performance, then the conclusion may not be reasonable.

Every reason is usually supported by at least one assumption. If the assumption is reasonable, the conclusion will also be reasonable.

Let's look at a few more examples:

Reason: I enjoyed this Stephen King book.

Conclusion: I will enjoy other books by Stephen King.

Assumption: *All Stephen King books are similar.*

Reason: Jill was caught stealing from the company.

Conclusion: Jill will be fired.

Assumption: *Stealing from the company is sufficient grounds for dismissal.*

Reason: The city council voted to cut city taxes.

Conclusion: City workers will be laid off.

Assumption: *The only way to save the money lost in taxes will be to reduce the payroll.*

Whenever we examine an argument, we need to identify any assumptions that are critical to the reasoning. Let's examine the following argument in paragraph form:

> The state legislature has proposed a requirement for Planned Parenthood, requiring teenagers to obtain parental permission before being given birth control information or assistance. This is a good idea because parents need to be involved to give the teens guidance and love when they are making such an important decision.

If we diagram the reasoning, we'll get something that looks like this:

> R1: Parents should be involved when teens make an important decision like whether to use birth control.

> C: Agencies who provide birth control information and assistance should be legally required to notify parents when their teens ask for birth control assistance.

This may seem like a reasonable argument, but the writer is making a rather large assumption: that all parents are willing and able to provide appropriate guidance and support for their teens. If the writer did not make this assumption, then the argument would not make sense. Let's look at this diagram again, but this time we'll add the assumption:

R1: Parents should be involved when teens make an important decision like whether to use birth control.

[A1: All parents are able and willing to provide appropriate guidance and support for their teens.]

C: Agencies who provide birth control information and assistance should be legally required to notify parents when their teens ask for birth control assistance.

Is the assumption warranted? In some cases, perhaps, but in many cases, the parents and the teens may be unable to discuss such an emotional issue because the level of communication between the parents and child is too low. Therefore, this argument is deficient.

Notice that arguments provide **hidden, or unstated,** reasoning in an argument. To identify assumptions, we need to look between the lines to figure out what ideas the author has not stated but are essential to the meaning of the argument.

Let's examine another argument:

The federal government should put more stringent gas mileage standards on automobiles. We don't have an endless supply of crude oil, and the more we use, the more hydrocarbons get into the atmosphere.

To diagram this argument, we need to add three assumptions the arguer is obviously making:

R1: We do not have an endless supply of crude oil.

R2: The more crude oil we use, the more hydrocarbons get into the atmosphere.

[A1: Hydrocarbons pollute the atmosphere.]

[A2: Automobiles consume crude oil in the form of gasoline.]

[A3: It is the role of the federal government to reduce pollution.]

C: The federal government should put more stringent gasoline mileage standards on automobiles.

The first and second assumptions are obviously warranted. Whether or not you agree with the third assumption depends on how you view the role of the federal government. This is a value assumption that is a matter of opinion; therefore, not everyone would agree with it. Unless you find all the assumptions valid, you will not find the argument sound.

Let's look at another:

> Students' SAT scores are lower today than they were twenty years ago. We need to increase the amount of money we are spending on education.

If we diagram this argument, adding the assumptions, this is what we have:

> R1: Students' SAT scores are lower today than they were twenty years ago.
>
> [A1: SAT scores are a good indicator of how much students are learning.]
>
> [A2: Students learn more if we spend more money on education.]
>
> C: We need to increase spending on education.

These assumptions may not be accurate. Many educators believe such standardized tests, while useful, do not give a complete picture of how much students have learned. We also know that money, by itself, will not guarantee improvement. It may be necessary to spend more money, but a better argument needs to be made.

Let's examine another common argument:

> The biggest problem with the welfare system in this country is that we are paying some people to stay home when they should be working. A simple solution would be to require all welfare recipients to work for their monthly checks.

This is an often-heard argument, and obviously it has some merit, but the writer is making a couple of important assumptions.

> R1: Some people drawing welfare benefits are able to stay home and not work.
>
> [A1: These people are able to work.]
>
> [A2: There are available jobs for these people.]

C: All welfare recipients should be required to work for their money.

Not everyone is physically or mentally able to hold down a job, and there are not always enough jobs for those people willing to work. The author's assumptions are not always true; therefore, the argument is flawed.

In all of these examples, implicit assumptions are important building blocks in the arguments. Without these assumptions, the arguments would make no sense. Of course, when one of these implicit assumptions is unwarranted, that throws the credibility of the entire argument into question. Obviously, we cannot thoroughly consider the effectiveness of an argument if we have not identified and evaluated the assumptions the author is making.

Exercise 7.1

Diagram each of the following arguments, supplying the unstated assumption:

1) Don't vote for that candidate because he has not been honest about his draft record.

> *Sample:*
> *R: That candidate has not been honest about his draft record.*
> *C: Don't vote for that candidate.*
> *A: The candidate will probably lie about other things too.*

2) I have been sick for three days, but I can't go see the doctor because I only have fifteen dollars.

3) I don't want to be lost in class today, so I must get my assignment done.

4) Nuclear power plants should not be built because they produce radioactive waste which remains radioactive for 20,000 years.

5) The government should require all cars to be equipped with air bags because they save lives.

6) We're having company, so I'd better clean house.

7) I'd better stay home tonight because I've got an exam tomorrow.

8) There's too much violent crime today; we really need gun control.

9) I want to go to college so I can get a good job.

10) She's going to have trouble in school because she's been out of school for so long.

11) I should not have voted for him. Ever since he's been mayor, the streets are full of potholes.

12) We don't have to worry about snow ruining our trip. The weatherman on Channel 6 said we would only have flurries.

13) I can't use that computer. After all, I can't even program my VCR.

14) I am very angry. I told him to meet me at 2:00; now it's 2:45!

Exercise 7.2

Diagram each of the following arguments, supplying the unstated assumption:

1) John is reading a Islamic magazine. He must be a Muslim.

2) Sam must be angry with me. I greeted him this morning, but he barely spoke to me.

3) Candidate A is twenty-five points ahead in the polls with one week to go before the election. She is sure to win.

4) I failed my math exam. Now I'll fail the course for sure!

5) The legislature has cut the appropriation to our college by ten percent. Some professors will be laid off.

6) My son took the SAT's and did very poorly on them. Now he'll never get into college!

7) Two years ago I earned $15,000, last year I earned $20,000, and this year I earned $25,000. I guess I'll be earning $50,000 in just five years!

8) The phone is ringing, and it's 3 a.m. It must be bad news!

9) My favorite TV show will be cancelled because it finished very low in the ratings.

10) I feel a pain in my chest. I'm having a heart attack!

11) Oh no! I just finished painting the garage, and now it's starting to rain. I'll have to do the job all over again.

12) I see a married friend of mine in a restaurant dining with an attractive young woman who is not his wife. He must be having an affair.

13) I'm getting a sore throat; I must be getting a cold.

14) The company where I work manufactures parts for machine guns, and the Congress just voted to cut the defense budget. I will lose my job.

15) I had a fight with my girlfriend this morning. I guess our date is off for tonight.

16) John told me the movie was very offensive, so I will not go see it.

In the following exercises, (1) DIAGRAM the arguments (2) IDENTIFY and EXPLAIN any ambiguous words or phrases (3) EVALUATE the quality of the evidence, and IDENTIFY any unstated assumptions and EXPLAIN if you think they are reasonable:

7.3 Many mothers who work and put their children in daycare centers feel guilty. In reality, there is no reason to feel guilty. Children who are in daycare do very well, often better than those children who do not attend daycare. Daycare gives children an opportunity to learn to play with other children. They would not have this if they stayed at home. Also, daycare centers can provide excellent learning activities to promote cognitive development. This helps younger children when they are ready to attend school. And finally, when mothers take their children to daycare, they are able to earn more money, which can provide a much richer home environment. All in all, children in daycare centers make out very well compared to children who do not have this advantage.

7.4 It is clear from the evidence we have so far that silicone breast implants are not safe. Take the case of Gloria Schwinn. She had breast implants ten years ago. Last month she had to have them removed because she was developing inflammatory joint disease. This disease has been linked by a major university study to leaking silicone from breast implants. And, if they were so safe, why have a number of manufacturers of these devices withdrawn them from the market? Think about it. Silicone is a foreign substance. It is not naturally produced by our bodies. Silicone breast implants are just not safe!

7.5 The media has to take their share of responsibility for promoting violence in our society. Violence in television shows, and particularly in movies, is having the effect of sending the wrong messages to our children. Many films today feature sympathetic characters who intentionally kill people without showing any form of remorse. What kind of a message does this send to children? The violence that is shown is also unnecessarily graphic. I have seen films in which people are actually dismembered, and the viewers see blood spurting from gaping wounds on their bodies. Children who see a steady diet of this must become desensitized to it. It is then just a small step for them to think that the violence they cause is no big deal.

7.6 Once again, a young boxer has been struck down in his prime, the inevitable result of this savage, unnecessary sport. On October 22, Tony "Slam" Petrocelli died as a result of the knockout he took in a professional boxing match the previous week. He was knocked unconscious in the tenth round and never regained consciousness. It is well known that many well-known boxers like Muhammad Ali and Floyd Patterson have suffered brain damage. Sports should be for healthy recreation. If a sport causes brain damage and death, it is time to get rid of it! Boxing should be banned.

7.7 Although many people are against it, I believe that it makes sense to lower the drinking age from twenty-one to eighteen. After all, if our soldiers are old enough to go fight a war at eighteen, then they should be old enough to have a beer! They are already allowed to sign contracts and inherit property! Eighteen-year-olds are already drinking anyway. Having a law forbidding it is ridiculous because it's already being violated. In fact, it would be easier to enforce such a law. If teenagers knew they would be able to drink at eighteen, they'd know they wouldn't have to wait so long, and would be less likely to drink illegally.

Exercise 7.8
Forget the Fads– The Old Way Works Best
Newsweek September 30, 2002
Evan Keliher
(Used with permission)

I've never claimed to have psychic powers, but I did predict that the $500 million that philanthropist Walter Annenberg poured into various school systems around the country, beginning in 1993, would fail to make any difference in the quality of public education. Regrettably, I was right.

By April 1998, it was clear that the much-ballyhooed effort had collapsed on itself. A Los Angeles Times editorial said, " All hopes have diminished. The promised improvements have not been realized." The program had become so bogged down by politics and bureaucracy that it had failed to create any significant change.

How did I know this would be the result of Annenberg's well-intentioned efforts? Easy. There has never been an innovation or reform that has helped children learn any better, faster or easier than they did prior to the 20th century. I believe a case could be made that real learning was better served then than now.

Let me quote Theodore Sizer, the former dean of the Harvard Graduate School of Education and the director of the Annenberg Institute for School Reform, which received some of the grant money. A few years ago a reporter asked him if he could name a single reform in the last 15 years that had been successful. Sizer replied, "I don't think there is one."

I taught in the Detroit public-school system for 30 years. While I was there, I participated in team-teaching, supervised peer-tutoring programs and tussled with block scheduling plans. None of it ever made a discernible different in my students' performance. The biggest failure of all was the decentralization scheme introduced by a new superintendent in the early 1970's. His idea was to break our school system into eight smaller districts--each with its own board of education--so that parents would get more involved and educators would be more responsive to our students' needs. Though both of those things happened, by the time I retired in 1986 the number of students who graduated each year still hadn't risen to more than half the class. Two thirds of those who did graduate failed the exit exam and received a lesser diploma. We had changed everything but the level of student performance.

What baffles me is not that educators implement new policies intended to help kids perform better, it's that they don't learn from others' mistakes. A few years ago I read about administrators at a middle school in San Diego, where I now live, who wanted a fresh teaching plan for their new charter school and chose the team-teaching model. Meanwhile, a few miles away, another middle school was in the process of abandoning that same model because it hadn't had any effect on students' grades.

The plain truth is we need to return to the method that's most effective: a teacher in front of a chalkboard and a roomful of willing students. The old way is the best way. We have it from no less a figure than Euclid himself. When Ptolemy I, the king of Egypt, said he wanted to learn geometry, Euclid explained that he would have to study long hours and memorize the contents of a fat math book. The pharaoh complained that that would be unseemly and demanded a shortcut. Euclid replied, "There is no royal road to geometry."

There wasn't a shortcut to the learning process then and there still isn't. Reform movements like new math and whole language have left millions of damaged kids in their wake. We've wasted billions of tax-payers dollars and forced our teachers to spend countless hours in workshops learning to implement the latest fads. Every minute teachers have spent on misguided educational strategies (like building kids' self esteem by acting as "facilitators" who oversee group projects) is time they could have been teaching academics.

The only way to truly foster confidence in our students is to give them real skills--in reading, writing, and arithmetic--that they can be proud of. One model that incorporates this idea is direct instruction, a program that promotes rigorous, highly scripted interaction between teacher and students.

The physicist Stephen Hawking says we can be sure time travel is impossible because we never see any visitors from the future. We can apply that same logic to the subject of school reforms: we know they have not succeeded because we haven't seen positive results. But knowing that isn't enough. We should stop using students as lab rats and return to a more traditional method of teaching. If it was good enough for Euclid, it is good enough for us.

CHAPTER 8
Critical Thinking and Advertising

Advertising plays an important role in our capitalistic economy. Because every business has the opportunity to compete in a supposedly free environment, each must find a way to get the message about its products and services out to the buying public. The advertising that fills our mailboxes, clutters our roadways, weighs down our Sunday newspapers, and continually interrupts our television viewing is the price we must pay for our free market system. Think of how many times we are exposed to some sort of advertising during the course of an average day. From the moment we wake up to the blaring of a clock radio to the moment we click off the television at the conclusion of the late news, we are inundated with hyped messages urging us to buy products we neither want nor need.

Although we may not enjoy or appreciate the amount of advertising we are exposed to, it is considered an essential component of doing business in a free market economy and is probably here to stay. Despite what we may think as we are watching those endless commercials between the scenes of our favorite programming, advertising is very effective. When corporations plan advertising campaigns, they regularly plan to spend large amounts of money to ad agencies and to television networks, radio stations, and print media. The advertising business is a huge industry employing thousands of creative professionals who think of innumerable ways to persuade us to buy their product or service. They wouldn't keep it up if they were not generating more money than they were spending. In other words, advertising works! If it didn't, they wouldn't use it.

This brings us to an important principle: *Advertising affects us all whether we know it or not.*

No matter how much we dislike advertising, no matter how many times we ridicule it, we are affected by it. We may not consciously make decisions based on what we have read or seen in advertisements, but we are not immune to it. It so pervades our environment that we have become accustomed to the hype. It works on our attitudes and decisions in subtle, often unconscious ways. Most of us like to think we are affected very little, but advertisers know how effective their ads are.

Critical thinking provides us with the tools we need to be wise consumers and evaluate advertising more thoroughly. As we have discussed, the purpose of critical thinking is to find truth. Advertising, of course, is not intended to present us with truth. This brings us to a second important principle about advertising: *Advertising creates an illusion of truth.*

Advertisers work very hard to create this illusion. Ads often present facts in a misleading or self-serving way intended to make it appear something is true when, in fact, it may not be. For example, Slim Fast advertisements make it appear that permanent weight loss is easy and fast. Procter and Gamble works to create the impression that Crest toothpaste alone can make a significant difference in the prevention of tooth decay. The advertisers of Promise margarine imply that their product will go a long way toward preventing heart disease. In each of these examples, there is an element of truth, but the impression the ad tries to create is an exaggerated version of the "truth" they want us to believe.

Every year, advertisers spend tens of billions of dollars on television, radio, newspaper, and magazine advertising. The methods they use vary widely, but they all work to create an illusion of truth that will appeal to consumers. Sometimes the representation of the product is accurate; other times it is not. It is up to us to determine how much to believe. It may be tempting to dismiss all advertising as unreliable, but that would be an oversimplification. Some ads actually contain useful information, which can help us make an intelligent decision about a product. Others, of course, are misleading and border on outright misrepresentation.

Advertisers do have to work within the law. Under present laws, an advertiser cannot knowingly lie, but courts have upheld the rights of advertisers to be intentionally misleading, citing the "Buyer Beware" principle. This means that it is up to the consumer to read ads carefully, including the fine print, to determine what the ad is actually claiming. If a consumer is misled because she failed to read the ad carefully, then the advertiser cannot be held liable. So it is clearly up to the consumer to exercise critical thinking when considering advertised products or services.

How Advertisers Create the Illusion of Truth

Advertisers use a variety of methods to mislead consumers. Some of the methods they use manipulate logic to create the impression that they are making a claim that they cannot honestly make. Careful reading of the ad will reveal that the inferred claim is not actually stated. In this way, the advertiser remains on safe legal ground while misrepresenting the product or service.

Here are some of the principal methods advertisers use to appeal to consumers. (This material is based on material developed by Ralph Johnson and Anthony Blair in *Logical Self Defense*, New York: McGraw Hill, 1994):

       1. Weasel words
       2. Meaningless words
       3. Mysterious ingredients or technology
       4. False or misleading inferences
       5. Suppressed evidence
       6. Appeals to emotion

<u>Weasel words</u> enable an advertiser to stop just short of making an outright false claim. These are words like "help," "virtually," "as much as," "up to," and "can." Read the familiar advertising claims below both with and without the weasel words:

> Our toothpaste *helps* reduce tooth decay...
> Our cereal has *virtually* no sugar...
> Save *as much as* 50% at our going-out-of-business sale...
> You *can* earn *up to* $50,000 a year...

In each of these cases, the advertiser has used a weasel word to keep from making a false claim. The toothpaste helps prevent tooth decay, along with going to the dentist, regular brushing, and so on, but how much of the "help" is contributed by the toothpaste? The cereal has some sugar. You can save from one percent to fifty percent in the sale. The most you can earn is $50,000, but how likely is that?

<u>Meaningless words</u> have open-ended meanings so they really don't say anything. Look at these examples:

> Our company has a *tradition of excellence*...
> Saab is *an intelligent car* to drive...
> The new Toyota Celica is *boldly expressive*...

These words add no specific meaning. They are included solely to create an impression of the product, but the words are essentially meaningless.

<u>Mysterious ingredients or technology</u> have been claimed for products for decades. Again, some familiar examples:

> Certs has *Retsyn*...
> Clorets has *Actizol*...
> Lipton uses the patented *flo-thru tea bag*...

What are Retsyn and Actizol? What do they really add to the product? Does the specially designed tea bag make any difference in the brewing of the tea? Again, these are examples of words which create an impression but make little difference.

<u>False or misleading inferences</u>: Another common technique of advertisers is to indirectly make a claim they cannot directly substantiate. Advertisers will frequently avoid making a claim directly because they cannot prove it. Instead, they will make it easy for the consumer to infer a specific meaning: the meaning they clearly want the

consumer to get out of the ad. Advertisers, then, cannot be held directly responsible for any false claims because they did not state anything they could not prove.

This strategy is often used by weight loss companies in television ads. A typical such commercial features a very thin, very attractive model using the weight loss product or service being advertised. The clear inference of these ads is that anyone who purchases this product or service will look like this model. The ads do not actually claim that the consumer will look like this, or that they will lose, and keep off, X amount of weight, but the inference is clear and often believable to consumers eager to escape obesity.

To use another example, consider a Volvo ad that appeared in major newsmagazines. The ad pictured a handsome physician, his sport coat draped over his shoulder, getting into a Volvo outside of a hospital emergency room. The text of the ad states that this physician, after working in emergency rooms for twelve years, seeing many patients injured in automobile accidents, has "another" reason for driving a Volvo. The ad clearly infers that the physician has been able to see which cars are safer because he works in an ER and that he knows Volvos are safer. This claim is not actually made in the ad; it is inferred only. You can often expect advertisers to use this technique, trying to get consumers to infer a meaning that cannot actually be made directly. In general, remember that advertisers, if they can, will make specific claims for their product. When they resort to having you make the inference yourself, it's probably because they do not have enough evidence to back up the claim themselves.

Suppressed evidence: Sometimes advertisers will simply omit relevant information from the ad to create the impression that it does not exist.

One popular ad campaign for the American dairy industry featured a series of commercials showing people drinking milk and participating in athletic, recreational, and family activities. The actors were healthy looking, attractive people who looked as though they were happy and enjoying themselves. The ads always ended with the tag line: "Milk, it does a body good!" These ads were suppressing the evidence about health problems related to saturated fat in the diet. Whole milk is a major source of dietary fat and actually contributes to cardiovascular disease. Although milk does have some valuable nutrients, that's not the whole story.

Ads for cars also tend to suppress evidence in their advertising. When they advertise a price, it is often unclear to which model that price applies. When a consumer goes to a car dealer to ask about the vehicle, she is often faced with a significantly higher price. The information about how the price was calculated for the advertised vehicle has been suppressed from the ad, or listed in very small print that the consumer may not be able to read.

Appeals to emotion: An appeal to emotion is designed to win the consumer over by capitalizing on his emotions: love, anger, fear, pity, or jealousy, for example. All types of advertising rely heavily on this type of appeal, especially television commercials. Many of the most popular commercials feature heartwarming, emotional scenes involving families and friends that often have very little to do with the product being sold.

Many pharmaceutical ads on television, for example, feature scenes of families or couples engaging in emotionally-compelling activities usually unrelated or only indirectly related to the drugs' actual uses. Erectile dysfunction drugs often show attractive, couples in suggestive situations inferring that they are planning to engage in sex . These appeal directly to the audience's emotions.

 Another effective technique, related to the appeal to emotion, is the use of humor. This may be the single most common technique used in television advertising, and it is very effective. People will remember ads that make them smile. These ads are so prolific because they work, even though they usually give little or no useful information about the product.

Because we live a free enterprise society, we expect the hype and colossal claims of advertising. Although we don't expect advertisers to be "truthful," we think we can avoid the effects of misleading advertising. It's not always easy to do so, and we need to be careful to examine all ads carefully.

Let's examine some advertisements to identify some of these misleading techniques. The ads on the following three pages are similar to many national ads appearing in magazines and newspapers everyday.

Win the War Against Plaque With New *Millennium Technology!* Try the new

PLATINUM WHITE®

in the battle against *Plaque and Tartar!*

Why use 20th century technology when the new millennium has brought the most effective technological weapon in plaque removal? The new Platinum White® can remove virtually all fresh plaque from tooth surfaces. The patented "plaque sensor" uses 21st century technology to sense plaque and adjust the speed and power of over 800 rotating Durashine7 bristles, at speeds of up to 2400 rpm, to scour plaque away.

The American Dental association has suggested that plaque removal is necessary to prevent cavities and gum disease. Protect your smile with PLATINUM WHITE®

118

I've Never Looked Better!

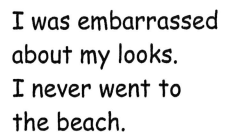

EASY SLIM®

has made a

difference

in my life!

I was embarrassed about my looks. I never went to the beach.

Now I look and feel great! And it was EASY With EASY SLIM®!

Studies show that Easy Slim® results in weight loss 95% of the time. Lose up to 5 pounds in the first week! Guaranteed to feel better and look better, or your money back.

Available at grocery and drug stores nationwide.

John wants to be around to see Katherine graduate from college.
So he takes a Heart Shield® Low-dose Aspirin every day!

Clinical Studies have demonstrated, again and again, that aspirin can help protect against heart attack. In fact, 4 out of 5 doctors recommend that high risk adults take an aspirin every day. And when it comes to aspirin, nothing works better than Heart Shield®. Why take chances with your future? Heart Shield®...the safety net you need.

PROTECT YOUR HEART.

Several misleading techniques are used in the PLATINUM WHITE ad. The most prominent is *mysterious technology*. This appears to be an electric toothbrush, but it is being sold as a high-tech alternative. What are the patented "plaque sensors"? What is the 21st century technology? What are "Durashine bristles"? The fact that is has 800 bristles and that they rotate at speeds "up to 2400 rpm" appeals to an irrational faith in technology. Note the use of *weasel words*. The claim that this device can remove "virtually" all "fresh" plaque," suggests it removes all plaque, but it does not say this. It removes not all but virtually all, and appears to concentrate on fresh or new plaque. What about the plaque that may have been around for awhile? Also the bristles rotate "up to" 2400 rpm." It could rotate much slower than that. The ad also uses a *misleading inference* by using the American Dental Association by name. It infers that the ADA endorses this product, but it does not actually state this. We can assume it does not. Finally, the ad uses *meaningless words*. What is "new millennium technology" and "21st century technology"? This ad gives us little useful information or evidence to suggest this product is superior.

The EASY SLIM ad relies heavily on *misleading inferences*. The before and after photographs clearly suggest that the user of EASY SLIM will achieve similar results, although the ad does not directly claim this. Since weight problems can cause emotional pain, this might also be considered an *appeal to emotion*, presuming that some of the readers might identify with the "before" picture. The ad also uses *suppressed evidence*. It gives no details about the studies conducted to demonstrate the weight loss "95% of the time." It also does not give much information about the guarantee. The ad wants to leave the impression that one will lose 5 pounds in a week, but the *weasel word* "up to" makes the claim meaningless.

Finally, the HEART SHIELD ad makes use of a clear *appeal to emotion* with the picture and the headline. Everyone fears being taken from their family by sudden death, and the illustration of the father and daughter, along with the suggestion in the headline, appeals to this fear. The ad also uses *suppressed evidence* by leaving out information about the clinical studies and the survey in which "4 out of 5 doctors recommend" low dose aspirin. The goal of the ad is to suggest that HEART SHIELD is superior to other forms of aspirin. By claiming that "nothing works better" than HEART SHIELD, the ad leaves the impression that HEART SHIELD is the best. This statement actually states that nothing performs better; that is because all aspirin performs equally well. This is a common example of a *misleading inference*.

Exercise 8.1

You will receive several print advertisements in class. Examine each of these ads for the techniques discussed in this handout. Identify any specific techniques and explain why each is misleading.

Exercise 8.2

Find an ad which you think uses one or more of these techniques. Explain why. Attach a copy of the ad to your assignment.

Exercise 8.3

Record a series of television commercials. Find one that you think uses some of the misleading advertising techniques discussed in this chapter. Bring the tape to class and be prepared to lead a discussion.

CHAPTER 9
Becoming a Critical Consumer of the News Media

One of the most remarkable technological developments of the twentieth century has been the increasing dominance of the electronic media. Every day we are bombarded with media messages that monopolize our cultural space. Almost every home has at least one television set; many have more. And the television sets are usually on, bringing a variety of programming and advertising into every living room. Elaborate cable and satellite systems make dozens of channels available, giving viewers worldwide an exceptional array of choices, from movies, to news programming, to sports events, to science and nature shows, to shopping networks, to specialty programming. Media is available to us literally twenty-four hours a day.

The advent of electronic media, and television in particular, has changed the way we process information. In the nineteenth century, before the beginning of this media revolution, information was experienced in a completely different way. Before the development of the telegraph, for example, the only way to get information from one area of the country to another was to physically carry it there, by train, by boat, or if one was in a hurry, by pony express. For this reason, information had to be of considerable importance to be sent across the country. Presidential election results and news about wars often took several weeks to reach everyone. People did not receive a large amount of information. Most of it was local or directly related to their lives.

The form of information was different as well. Most of the serious information available was in written form, which required people to read it. People were used to reading to get the information they needed. Neil Postman has called this period the "typographic age" because of its reliance on the structure of written language. He makes the point that even politicians gave long, complex, speeches, but that the people were used to listening to them, because they were used to reading complicated prose. He cites the example of the public debates between Abraham Lincoln and Stephen Douglas, in their famous Senate debates of 1858, which often lasted five or six hours while people listened attentively (*Amusing Ourselves to Death: Public Discourse in the Age of Show Business*, 1985). It is impossible to imagine people today concentrating on what any politician has to say for more than thirty seconds. The average sound bite on the news is considerably shorter than that.

With the invention of the telegraph, it became possible to send a message across the country in a matter of seconds. This not only increased the timeliness of information, it also increased the amount of information. Newspapers were able to gather and print information about events occurring all over the country. People became more aware of what was going on in far away places. This trend accelerated with the development of "wireless telegraphy," soon to become known as radio. Now citizens could listen as the President took the oath of office and hear live reports from battle scenes in World War II. Information was rapidly becoming a sought-after commodity.

Advertisers started paying the cost to bring radio programs to every home, and the modern media age was upon us.

But how has this development of electronic media affected the way we process information? How has the electronic media, and television in particular, changed the way we look at information? Today, information is abundant. We have more information than we can possibly use. With so many ways to access information, our question has become not, "Where can I get the information I need?" but rather, "What does all this information mean?" We no longer need to be very literate to become a consumer of media. We can watch television all day and get plenty of information without reading. But what is this information for? How will we use the information? How will it affect our lives?

The purpose of this chapter is to explore the nature of the news media in particular. For our purpose, we will consider the news media to include television news, newspapers and magazines, radio, and the Internet.

So what about the information provided to us on the news media? Is it useful to us? Of course, some of it is. We need to decide for whom to vote. We need information about the weather so we can plan our activities. We often learn about issues that affect our health. Some of what we get from the news media is very relevant to us. But most of it is not. It may be interesting for us to see a film about a typhoon in a faraway place, but it will not change the way we conduct our lives. Neither will stories about corruption in another state, peace in Northern Ireland, or a murder in a small California town.

In fact, the news media exists primarily to make money. This is true of all forms of media in our capitalistic culture. Newspapers and magazines would not exist if they were not able to sell a substantial amount of advertising. Television networks compete with one another for high ratings so they can charge their advertisers more money per minute for commercials. It's important to remember that it was not always this way. News proliferation was originally viewed as a way to keep the citizenry informed. During the American Revolution, for example, newspapers were considered essential to informing the public about the insurgency and about how the new republic would be governed. Publishers did not make money from these newspapers. They were happy to get enough money to pay the costs of publication. Even in the early days of television broadcasting, television news programs were brief, and considered a public service. It cost television stations more money to produce the news than they made in revenue. News was considered a money-losing proposition.

This all changed gradually as media became more competitive and was increasingly controlled by large corporations whose goal it was to make money. So the role of the news media has changed from a public service designed to inform the citizenry to more of an entertainment medium designed to keep us reading and watching. Television news programs will do whatever is necessary to keep the audience watching. The stories they present, the images they show, are all designed with one purpose in mind: to make sure we don't change the channel. So, these programs make sure to entertain, to present programming that appeals to the viewers. They don't want to risk being boring or dry, not when their advertising rates are directly tied to the number of people watching.

As critical thinkers, we need to become good consumers of the news. We need to understand what we are seeing and reading, and be able to use the information we receive to make sound judgments. To do this, we need to examine television news, print news, radio, and the Internet in more detail.

Television News

Television news, including local news broadcasts, network news shows, and cable news channels, is, by far, the dominant form of news media at the beginning of the 21st century. The availability of news on the Internet is becoming an increasingly potent force in presentation of news, but it is primarily sponsored by the same large corporations, which produce news for the mainstream broadcast and print media. The fact remains, most people still get their news from television.

When television began to appear in large numbers in American homes, in the early 1950's, television news programming was very brief and not profitable. A majority of American people claimed to get their news primarily from newspapers. Evening newspapers flourished in most American cities. This changed as television broadcasters began expanding their news organizations. The first network television news broadcast was *The Camel News Caravan*, hosted by John Cameron Swayze, and was fifteen minutes long. Walter Cronkite hosted the first thirty minute network news broadcast the, *CBS Evening News*, in 1963. (Campbell et. al. *Media and Culture*, 2004). The half-hour network news broadcast remained the centerpiece of national television news broadcasting until 1980, when Ted Turner started the Cable News Network (CNN) dedicated to providing twenty-four hour news coverage seven days a week. CNN was soon joined by MSNBC, a joint twenty-four hour cable news venture between NBC and Microsoft, and a third twenty-four hour news channel, Fox News. Viewers now have access to television news at any time of the day. The network news divisions, as well as the twenty-four hour cable news channels are all extremely competitive and are required to show a profit. This obviously affects the content and format of the programming. Needless to say, virtually all major evening newspapers have disappeared, and morning newspapers, as we will discuss later, have adapted to the television age.

It is increasingly important that we become informed and literate consumers of news programming. Simply watching the news is not a good way to stay informed and get the information we need to make intelligent decisions as a citizen in our republic. As in other areas of critical thinking, we need to work harder than just passively watching these programs. To do this, it's important to understand several fundamental facts about television news. Keeping each of these ideas in mind when we are watching this programming will enable us to see television news for what it is, with its obvious benefits along with its severe limitations.

Television News Is Primarily Entertainment

The commercial television networks won't tell you this, but television news is designed to entertain. It does, in fact, inform the public, but it doesn't do this very well, as we will see, and informing is secondary to entertainment. The reason for this is very understandable. Corporate television networks exist to make a profit, and they must do so in an extremely competitive environment. Viewers have many choices for television news, so if they become bored or otherwise dissatisfied with the channel they are watching, they can easily switch channels. So, not surprisingly, the television networks try hard to hold viewers. This has a number of implications for news broadcasts.

First, it affects the nature of the stories covered. Some stories are naturally more interesting to viewers than others. Stories that affect them directly, like weather and consumer alerts, tend to be interesting. Foreign news, unless it's very dramatic or affects our country directly, is not interesting to many American viewers. Very sensational stories that depict disasters or contain exciting visuals are, of course, interesting. Detailed analysis of public policy issues, like taxation or federal agricultural policies, are boring to most viewers. It's easy to see that some types of stories, no matter how important, simply don't get covered with much detail.

Second, it affects the news broadcast itself, which must appear to be very dramatic to hold the viewers. For this reason, these programs begin with urgent music and bold use of graphics to get the viewers' attention immediately. The broadcast often begins with previews, not unlike movie previews, which urge the viewer to "stay tuned," to see these upcoming stories. Even the on-air personalities are groomed to make the news entertaining. They are good-looking and pleasant. The women are generally young and attractive. They cultivate the friendly image so we will invite them into our homes every evening, almost as a part of the family. Everything in the news broadcast is designed with one goal: to keep us watching.

There are several notable exceptions to this tendency to make the news a form of entertainment. Both the Public Broadcasting System and C-Span provide news coverage in a serious format. Notably, PBS's *The News Hour* provides in-depth analysis of a few major stories each evening. It does not rely as much on visuals but more on analysis and commentary. C-Span's format is unique, and it specializes in broadcasting live government-related events without commentary. Although the cable news networks have twenty-four hours to fill, and tend to do a good job covering breaking news like the September 11, 2001 terrorist attacks, they still cover a good deal of "soft" news and try to make their stories as entertaining as possible.

The Coverage of Stories on Television News is Superficial

We rarely get in-depth analysis of stories on television news. It's easy to see why. Consider a half-hour news broadcast. Out of the thirty minutes, usually at least ten minutes consist of commercials. That leaves less than twenty minutes for news stories. Each story must be brief, often very brief. This promotes superficial coverage. After all, how much can you really say about a story in a minute or two? For this reason, a news broadcast is comparable to a series of headlines rather than any type of in-depth analysis. Even on cable news programs, the length of individual stories is short; they don't want to risk boring the viewers who might be motivated to switch channels.

You might try this for yourself. The next time you watch a news broadcast, count how many stories you view in a half-hour of broadcast time. You may note a total of ten to fifteen stories reported during that time frame, some less than one minute long. Obviously, such stories cannot provide any significant depth.

So is this a problem? Not really, as long as we know what we're getting: an entertaining, mildly informative program. The problem is that the media hype can lull us into believing we ARE informed. The advertising surrounding the news can easily leave us with the impression that news is serious business, and that news programs exist to keep us up-to-date and informed. This is just not true. They exist to make money by selling advertising and keeping us watching. Informing the citizenry is secondary at best.

Television News is Primarily a Visual Medium

What distinguishes television from other forms of media is the moving image. This is the characteristic of television news which makes it most compelling. We can actually *see* what is happening. We can see the agony of victims of a disaster. We can see an impeachment actually being debated. We can even see a war in progress with people dying. This is very powerful and is why television has become the dominant format for news.

The fact that television news is very visual is obvious. The effects of this may not be so obvious. Perhaps the most significant effect of this is that images overwhelm words. When we are watching images on a screen, we tend to focus our concentration on the images. If words are being spoken by the people on the screen, we may pay some attention to that. But, as is often the case with television news, a voice is speaking over the image, we tend to focus on the image. We often do not hear the words. They just go by. We may *think* we're paying attention, but often we're not. The problem is that thinking requires language and analysis. If we are not hearing the words, no matter how eloquent they are, we're missing the point. The image becomes the point.

Good examples of the power of images to affect the viewer are the dramatic television images of the September 11, 2001 terrorist attacks. In fact, the terrorists who planned and carried out this attack understood the power of images to shape a reaction to an event. They undoubtedly knew that all television cameras would be trained on the towers after the first plane flew into one tower. Thus, the horrifying impact of the second plane flying into the second power was televised live to a stunned television audience. Those images were played and replayed on television as the world watched in horror. The terrorists knew that the effect of the attacks would be greater because of these images, and they were.

Another more historical example of the power of the television image to affect a story involved the 1960 televised debates between John F. Kennedy and Richard Nixon. Although the viewers who listened to the debate on radio thought Nixon had won the debate, the television pictures told another story. Nixon looked tired and humorless on television and sported a heavy five o'clock shadow. Kennedy appeared young and vigorous, and most viewers of the debate thought he had done a better job. In the close 1960 presidential election, these images arguably made the difference. Today, presidential candidates concentrate on their televised image; they know it may make or break their campaigns.

Another problem is that an image is not reality. A video clip of an event is not the same as the event itself. News producers consciously decide what footage to show of a particular event. They do this to emphasize what they want to show, usually what will be most compelling for the viewer. This is called "framing." The news frames the story, presents it in a particular context that defines the issues for the viewer. We cannot see what the news producer has left out. We are forced to rely on their final product. We essentially have to trust them to present the story in a fair and objective manner that accurately represents the reality. Take, for example, the story of rioting that may be occurring in a particular city. The news organizations, wanting to create as much viewer interest as possible, will frame the story as a major conflict and may leave the impression with viewers that the entire city is engulfed in violence. The fact may be that only one or two neighborhoods may be involved, but the continuous, dramatic coverage may leave another impression. The news programs will not show the peaceful portions of the city; there's no news there. But that, in itself, is misleading. The news producers are concentrating more on keeping us watching than on presenting the most objective reality. As critical thinkers, we need to understand this. We can't rely just on what we see.

Remember, when we watch the images of a news event on television, we are only seeing a small fraction of what really took place. We are limited to what the photographer decided to shoot, most of which does not even make it into the story. Perhaps an hour of video was shot to make a one- to two- minute story. The editor can frame the story in a particular way to make a particular point. So when we see the story, we're just getting a very small fragment of the overall story designed to emphasize what the editors have decided is important, or more likely, what the editors think will keep us from changing the channel.

Television News Emphasizes Conflict Over Substance

Television news programming concentrates on conflict because it is often more interesting to viewers than substance. A good example of this is the coverage of presidential debates. The networks always provide extensive coverage of these events, and they almost always frame them in terms of who won, who lost, who scored points, and who had the best strategy. Very little, if any, discussion centers on the policy issues debates or the candidates' stands on the issues. Not surprisingly, the candidates understand this and try to produce sound bites for the news programs, because that's what will be reported after the debate. The candidate who delivers the best one-liner, no matter how irrelevant, will make the news broadcast.

The press often concentrates on election strategy and conflict to the exclusion of substantive issues. This, again, is understandable. If the primary goal of television news is to keep us watching, conflict does the job. Not only does it provide good drama, but it keeps us primed for the next installment. After all, if Candidate A blew his chance to score points in this debate, we should stay tuned to see if he can recover in next week's debate. It is not unlike the appeal of a sports event.

This "conflict" framing of the news carries over to other topics which are even less related to the competitive nature of campaigns. When a particular piece of legislation is being proposed by the Republicans, for example, the press almost immediately focuses on whether the Republicans will prevail, or whether the Democrats will be able to "beat" the Republican proposal. Very little air time is devoted to the actual merits of the particular proposal. Often no discussion is devoted to the "context" of the issue so the viewers can understand the logic behind the proposal. Pay attention to the coverage of politics, and you'll see how this works. Unfortunately, the effect is often to make the public cynical and disillusioned about politics. No matter what the politicians say, the media tries to turn it into a competitive contest, and the public gets disgusted and tunes it out. It is a significant problem for our democracy.

Television News Is Not Objective

Finally, it's important to realize that television news does not just objectively report the facts. First of all, that goal is difficult to achieve with any media. By deciding what to report and what to omit, a reporter or correspondent is automatically framing the news in a particular way. But television news is particularly biased. The bias is not so much a liberal or conservative bias, although they have been accused of that, but a bias of focusing on what will make viewers keep tuning in.

Although the medium is primarily a visual one, we do need to pay close attention to the use of language to understand this bias. Rarely does the television reporter simply explain what happened. More often, the reporter uses language to frame the story, to put it into some context. The language does not just state facts, it analyzes and makes inferences.

For example, Bernard Goldberg, has accused the major American media, and CBS News in particular, of using biased language to report the news. In his 2002 book, *Bias: A CBS Insider Exposes How the Media Distort the News,* Goldberg uses an example from a story on the *CBS Evening News* on Steve Forbes' flat tax proposal reported by Eric Engberg. At one point in the story Engberg uses the following words (underlining added): "Steve Forbes <u>pitches</u> his flat tax <u>scheme</u> as an economic <u>elixir,</u> good for everything that ails us." These words clearly reflect a negative bias towards the plan by the reporter.

Here's another example: from *NBC Nightly News* on December 30, 1999, the day before New Year's Eve 2000, when the world was fearful of the Y2K computer bug (italics added):

> **Tom Brokaw**: From the beginning, some of the most acute concerns about Y2K difficulties involved air travel which, after all, is heavily reliant on computers. It's one thing to stock up on bottled water and canned food, but if *something goes wrong in mid-flight, there aren't a lot of home remedies.* NBC's Robert Hager joins us now from Reagan National Airport in Washington. Robert, what's the latest?
> **Robert Hager**: Well, Tom, *the government swears* it's expecting no problems in this country, but millions of passengers are voting with their feet staying away from airports like this as the clock ticks over. Just today, *the FAA confesses* finding and fixing a previously undiscovered Y2K computer problem, that problem, in a back-up to a back-up system of twenty computers nationwide that track passenger planes at cruise altitudes. The union that services the computers says it could have *caused trouble.*
> **Professor Chris Primeau of Airways Systems Specialists**: Potentially it was a *very serious problem.* It's possible all the controllers could have lost all their data information and not known which plane was which.
> **Robert Hager**: But the FAA says it would take a highly unusual double failure right at midnight to cause, at worst, a ten second delay... But the big story that passengers are staying away, and, left with empty seats, the airlines are suddenly canceling even more flights than normal, tomorrow canceling 80% of regular Friday flights. Travel agents say *most of their clients are too worried to book<u>...</u>*

It is clear from this example that the network was framing this story to alarm viewers when, in fact, there was very little evidence that there was a serious problem with air traffic, and, in fact, there was information to the contrary. But the story was more compelling framed in this way. We have to wonder whether the passengers' fears were actually caused by this media hype over the Y2K problem. The irony of this example is that the media may have been reporting on a story actually created by their own biased coverage. Unfortunately, this type of example is not unusual.

Another way in which television news is not objective is in its choice of what to include in a story and what to leave out. In the CBS flat tax story that Goldberg referred to, he also pointed out that Engberg interviewed three tax experts about the proposal, and all three opposed the tax plan. The reporter chose to present these experts, even though there were others who supported the flat tax proposal.

When the American television networks reported on the Iraq War in 2003, most of the stories focused on the American soldiers and the technological superiority of the United States military. Reporters, who were "embedded" with American troops, naturally reported the war from the American perspective. The progress of the troops and the number of American casualties were meticulously reported. The number of Iraqi casualties and the effect of the war on Iraqi civilians was not included in most American television reports. Not surprisingly, the Arab television networks, like Al Jazeera, reported the war from the Iraqi perspective, reporting the deaths of Iraqi civilians and the brutality of the American attack. Just deciding what stories make the news is a decision that is not objective.

In many ways, the media, particularly television, decide what the major issues of the day will be simply by deciding what to cover. If the television networks pick up a story, the politicians must respond. The issues that the networks do not cover receive very little attention. This biased selection may not be intended to set the agenda for national discussion, but that's exactly what happens.

As critical thinkers, we need to remind ourselves that we are not seeing all there is to see when we watch television news. The news is being analyzed, framed, and interpreted for us. It is not just being laid out for us to draw our own conclusions. The language used is designed to make the news dramatic, to tell a compelling story, and ultimately to entertain. We need to keep this in mind.

Print News Media

The print news media, although they have been eclipsed somewhat by television news, still provide an essential alternative for those who are seeking accurate, in-depth information. The primary difference between television and print media is the format. Whereas on television, the viewer has no control over the depth or sequence of the news presentation, in a newspaper or magazine, the reader has the opportunity to select which story to read, how much of it to read, and the ability to reread it if necessary. For this reason, print media can offer more depth and variety than television. Television has to create a show that will appeal to everyone. A newspaper, for example, can appeal to a wide variety of readers who will each read different portions of the newspaper. This allows newspapers to cover stories in more depth than television.

Print news, in other respects, suffers from some of the same problems as television news. It also has to keep readers interested. Because more viewers are used to watching television, and have a shorter attention span, the newspapers have had to spruce up their image to appeal to visually-oriented readers. Newspapers use more color and eye-catching graphics today than ever before. They run quite a few consumer-interest and feature news stories that are designed to please readers. In some newspapers, in-depth analysis of dry policy issues is dropped in favor of additional advertising or more interesting, perhaps less important, topics.

Newspapers and newsmagazines share one very common characteristic with television news: they focus on conflict. Newspapers and newsmagazines frame their stories around the battles and winners and losers because it creates more compelling copy. Like television news, *Newsweek* and *Time* find conflict irresistible. And, like television news, they are far from objective. The language used to prepare the stories reads much more like commentary than objective reporting of the facts.

If our goal, as critical thinkers, is to stay informed, then print media provide a useful supplement to television news. There are many newspapers and magazines, published in the United States and abroad, which can provide excellent information. A number of large, comprehensive newspapers, like *The New York Times, The Los Angeles Times, The Boston Globe, The Philadelphia Inquirer, The Wall Street Journal, The Chicago Tribune,* and *The Washington Post* are available nationally, and on-line, which provide detailed coverage of world affairs unlike any coverage available on television. The most common newsweeklies include *Time, Newsweek,* and *US News and World Report.* Additionally, many specialty magazines provide news-related commentary, including such publications as *The Atlantic Monthly, Harper's, The New Yorker, The National Review, and The New Republic.*

For the thinker who wants to stay informed, the print media provides perhaps the best alternative. It is certainly not as timely as television, but often far more thorough.

Radio News

Before the advent of television, radio was the primary vehicle for delivering timely news to the world. Americans received much of their news about World War II from live radio broadcasts. The legendary Edward R. Murrow pioneered the immediacy of the live broadcast by reporting from war-torn London during the Nazi bombardment of Britain.

Today, radio is usually reserved for entertainment, mostly music. There are two major exceptions to this, however: talk radio, and National Public Radio. Some metropolitan areas also feature stations with an all news format, although these stations tend to provide brief stories repeated frequently for listeners commuting to work and do not provide much in-depth analysis.

Talk radio, frequently broadcast on AM stations, has provided a forum for commentary and listener talk on a variety of subjects. Because the costs of producing a radio show is not nearly as expensive as putting on a television broadcast, many of these talk shows are free of corporate ownership and influence. The hosts on these shows frequently bring extreme or out-of-the-mainstream views to their commentaries and usually reflect a narrow range of conservative opinion. This is not really an example of news broadcasting. It is more a form of commentary, which has had an influence on public affairs because it often attracts listeners with strong views and provides a public forum for them to air their views.

National Public Radio has emerged as a serious competitor to television and print media as a news outlet. Because of the radio format, NPR can offer the type of in-depth analysis television often cannot. It provides serious, thoughtful commentary throughout the day and often covers stories not easily covered by television. Because it is non-commercial, NPR does not have as much pressure to keep a large number of listeners as commercial television.

The Internet

The emergence of the Internet in the 1990's was clearly the most significant development in news proliferation since the development of television. Although it has not supplanted television as the primary medium, it is providing serious competition for the print media. In fact, most television networks and print publications are using the Internet as a primary form of distribution, at least in an abridged format.

In some significant ways, the Internet combines the best of television and the print media. It is timely but also provides more depth and breadth of coverage. It is provides news on demand. Unlike any other media, it provides comprehensive information on any subject immediately accessible to anyone with a computer. It is very cheap to access, at least at the moment, and it allows the user to control exactly what information is accessed. For example, if the user is interested in learning about a regional war in Syria she can read news reports from major news outlets, visit sites within Syria and other Middle Eastern nations, and even read the views of refugees and other special interest groups at their propaganda sites. Never before has the comprehensive array of information been so available, so easily, as it is today.

But there are problems. In the case of television and radio, the Federal Communication Commission regulates all broadcasting and enforces standards. No agency regulates the Internet. As a result, much of the information available on the Internet is unreliable. Some of it is outright false. More often, Web sites which look like authentic news or information sites are actually fronts for commercial purposes. The information may be accurate, but incomplete or skewed in some way, which enhances its commercial purpose. For example, a manufacturer or distributor for an herbal digestive remedy might put up a site that purports to be an information site providing information to people with digestive problems. In fact the information is there only to sell their product, and may be medically unreliable, even dangerous. There is no outside agency supervising the accuracy of this type of information. No one holds Internet sites accountable like other news media outlets.

Being able to evaluate an Internet site is an increasingly important media-literacy skill. The most obvious precaution we can take as Internet users is to be sure the organization offering the site is reputable. Fortunately, most news-related sites are sponsored by major news outlets like, CNN, *The New York Times, USA Today,* and MSNBC. Most college and university library web pages contain excellent guidelines for evaluating Internet sites.

Staying informed is not easy. Never before have we had access to so much information. But, as we have seen, having access to information does not always mean we have the information we need to make good decisions. It's still difficult to be an informed consumer of the news, and, like other aspects of critical thinking, requires an investment of time and energy.

Exercise 9.1

For this exercise, videotape and watch a network news broadcast:

    a. List all the stories covered, and the duration, in minutes, of each.

    b. List all the commercials contained in the news broadcast.

    c. Select one story you want to examine in depth:

        1) Transcribe one minute of that story. (Write it out, word for word)

        2) Describe the visuals used in the story.

        3) Examine what you have, and answer the following questions:

            –How did the broadcast "frame" this story? What was the conflict? Explain, using specific examples from the story.

            –Did the reporter just report the facts, or did he or she interpret these fact for the viewer. Explain.

            –Why do you think the news director chose these visuals? Explain.

    d. The day AFTER the news broadcast, buy a nationally distributed newspaper like *The New York Times, USA Today, or The Washington Post.*

        1) Examine the length of coverage of any of the television stories you can find in the newspaper. List the length of each story in column inches. (A column inch is one column of print one inch long. Some stories stretch over two or more columns.)

        2) Compare the depth of coverage by the newspaper of these stories with the TV version. Were any of these stories "framed" differently in the newspaper? Explain.

            –Why do you think some TV stories did not show up in the newspaper.

            –List the stories you consider important that did not appear in the TV news.

    e. Can you make any connection between what you discovered in this assignment and our study of critical thinking? Explain, using specific critical thinking concepts from the text.

Exercise 9.2

Watch and record approximately one hour of national news broadcasts. You may use regular network broadcasts (ABC, CBS, or NBC) and/or cable news broadcasts (CNN, MSNBC, or Fox News). Avoid local news broadcasts and newsmagazine programs like *Dateline* or *60 Minutes.*

See if you can find evidence in any of these broadcasts of the following points about television news discussed in this chapter:

- Television news is primarily entertainment.
- The coverage of stories on television news in superficial.
- Television news is primarily a visual medium.
- Television news emphasizes conflict over substance.
- Television news is not objective.

Use specific quotes and examples from the news broadcast to support your points.

If you can, bring your videotape to class, cued up to a portion of the video you might use to illustrate a particular point. Be prepared to share your observations with the class.

APPENDIX I
Guidelines for Preparing Written Commentaries of Arguments

A commentary is a written critique of an argument. Preparing an effective commentary requires that we clearly understand the arguer's reasoning and are able to use critical thinking skills to assess its effectiveness. Before getting into the details of preparing a commentary, it is important to keep several things in mind:

1. No argument is perfect. It is unlikely that any argument we read will cover all the bases and provide absolute proof to substantiate all its reasons. Nevertheless, some arguments are clearly more effective than others. Our goal is to identify the primary strengths and weaknesses of the argument and suggest areas for improvement.

2. Everyone is not going to agree. Arguments are not open to absolute interpretations. Arguments are made up of language, which always can be interpreted differently by different readers. We all have different experiences, which will color our view of an argument. These different views will become obvious as we discuss arguments in class. Your goal, in preparing a commentary, is to make a reasonable case for your assessment of the argument. It should be clearly written and use substantial support from the argument itself. It does not matter whether your commentary agrees, in every aspect, with other students' assessments. As a class, however, we will likely reach broad agreement about many aspects of the argument.

3. Be generous; don't attack the argument on a technicality. We are evaluating the intended reasoning of the author. We need to read the argument in the fairest way possible. If the author wrote a portion of her argument in an unclear way, but it is clear from the context what she meant, evaluate her intended meaning. Don't reject the reasoning because the author made an obvious language error.

4. Try to separate your opinion about the issue from the commentary itself. You might, for example, agree with the author's point but determine that the author's reasoning is not sound. Conversely, you might strongly disagree with the conclusion but find the reasoning to be good. *Remember, you are evaluating the quality of the reasoning, not the desirability of the conclusion.*

The commentary is a written analysis of the reasoning in the argument.
It is not necessary to include a diagram of the reasoning in the argument commentary. It is, however, a good idea to construct a diagram, for yourself, to use to help focus on the specific reasons the arguer is using. Further, working on the diagram will help you distinguish between the reasons and the conclusion.

The following elements should be included in your written commentary of an argument:

1. CONCLUSION: State, in one complete sentence, the author's conclusion. Remember, it may be directly stated anywhere in the argument (beginning, middle or end), OR it may not be stated directly, but only inferred.

2. ASSESSMENT OF THE REASONING:

Ambiguity: As discussed in Chapter 5, the first step in evaluating the effectiveness of the argument is to determine if any of the reasons, or the conclusion, are ambiguous. Serious ambiguity in an argument makes an argument weak because the reader cannot be sure what the author is arguing.

Identify any ambiguous words or phrases. *Be sure to put ambiguous words or phrases in quotation marks* so it is easy determine exactly which words in the argument you are referring to. Clearly explain why these words or phrases are ambiguous.

Evidence: The evaluation of the evidence may be the lengthiest portion of the commentary. Chapter 6 outlines, in detail, what types of evidence tend to be used in arguments. When evaluating the quality of the evidence, consider the following questions:

> Does this reason need any evidence for support, or is it self-evident?

> If the reason requires evidence, is enough provided? Does it support the reasoning well?

> Does this evidence sound reasonable?

> Can such evidence easily be verified?

> If the evidence is not easy to believe, has the author listed sources?

Explain if the evidence presented in the argument is clear and convincing. Remember, when discussing evidence, you are doing two things: (a) evaluating whether the arguer used sufficient, high quality evidence, and (b) pointing out what specific type of additional evidence would be required to make the argument credible.

Assumptions:. Identify any important *implicit* (unstated) assumptions the author is making in the argument. Chapter 7 gives guidelines for identifying assumptions. You need to do two things: (a) state each assumption clearly, and (b) explain if you consider the assumption to be reasonable and why.

Implications: Presume, for the sake of this section, that the arguer has made a valid point, and that we should follow his or her reasoning, and adopt the arguer's position. What might we reasonably expect the implications, or consequences, of this to be? What effects might we see immediately or down the road? For each implication, explain whether this would be desirable or undesirable.

For example, let's presume you are reading an argument that suggests that all welfare recipients who refuse to work be cut off from all further government assistance. This may have some good reasoning to support it, but we'd also need to consider the consequences, or implications of such a policy. It is possible that some positive consequences might occur. If recipients knew they had to work, they might get jobs and become self–sufficient. This would be a desirable outcome. On the other hand, if the recipients were unable to find work, or were unable to work for some reason, the outcome could be devastating. Families could be left without any source of income. Crime might be expected to increase. Children in those families could suffer from malnutrition or disease.

In any event, a thorough evaluation of the argument must, necessarily, include an examination of the implications of the reasoning. If the implications are generally positive, this would indicate that the argument may be effective. The presence of many negative implications could indicate that the argument is incomplete or needs more development.

Bias or expertise: From what you can determine about the author's qualifications, job, or background, assess (a) whether the author has any built-in bias toward the subject, and (b) whether you believe the author has the necessary expertise to address this subject. Of course, you may not know much about the author from what is revealed in the argument, so you may not be able to make much of assessment. If the author is representing an organization, you may be able to check the goals and agenda of the organization by going online.

It is important to consider whether or not the author might have any emotional, financial, or other stake in getting us to believe his argument. For example, assume you are reading an argument about oat bran, which suggests that this is an extremely healthy food, but the author works for the Quaker Oats Company. You might suspect that his argument might be biased in favor of his employer, and that he might be overstating the benefits of eating oat products.

Some authors might be affected by emotional considerations. For example, let's assume that a father who had been through a long, bitter legal battle for the custody of his children wrote an argument favoring more legal rights for fathers in child custody cases. His argument might be considered biased to the extent that he had been through a presumably emotional experience involving this issue, and his bitterness might affect his objectivity. On the other hand, he might have gained some valuable firsthand knowledge about the way the system works. But, nonetheless, we would need to consider the possibility that he would be biased.

Expertise can be difficult to assess, although, we are often able to determine if the author has applicable education or work experience. As with bias, information obtained online from a search engine might be useful in assessing an author's expertise.

3. SUGGESTIONS FOR IMPROVING THE ARGUMENT: Your final task in the commentary is to make specific suggestions as to how the argument might be improved. In other words, if you were going to construct an argument to support the same conclusion, how might you improve it? Suggested improvements might include the following:

Adding reasoning that you think might make the argument stronger.

Including additional evidence that would provide better support for particular reasons.

Clarifying ambiguity in specific reasons.

Omitting portions of the argument that you do not consider effective.

It is important to explain *why* each suggestion will help make the argument more effective.

A good commentary should provide a clear analysis of the quality of the author's reasoning. It should refer to specific parts of the reasoning and be specific and to the point. Appendix II and Appendix III provide examples of well-written commentaries.

APPENDIX II
Sample Commentary

Don't Support Animal Experimentation
Dr. Alfred Love

Before you just blindly give to medical charities, consider the fact that most of them condone cruel animal experimentation. In fact, last year alone, the American Heart Association spent nearly $51 million on research. Most of that money was spent on experiments involving the use of animals. This respected organization has a history of starving, freezing, and torturing defenseless animals. The American Cancer Society annually spends millions of dollars on research, mostly injecting poor animals with tumor-causing viruses and testing chemotherapy agents on them. These experiments, besides being cruel, do not work. Animals do not have the same immune system that humans do, so whatever information the research produces is useless. In fact no new treatment for cancer has ever been developed through animal experimentation. The money could better be spent on clinical studies involving humans. The March of Dimes spent $43 million last year on research to prevent birth defects, again using animals for experimentation. Yet, the number of birth defects went up last year. Scientists have now developed computer models that make animal experimentation unnecessary! So rather than continue to support such cruel animal experimentation, donate your hard-earned dollars to Citizens for Humane and Effective Medical Research (CHEMR) today! We support organizations, which do not experiment on animals. Send your donations to CHEMR, P.O. Box 6384, Augusta, Maine 04330.

Dr. Love is a veterinarian and the executive director of the Citizens for Humane and Effective Medical Research (CHEMR).

The following is a good example of a commentary that might be prepared for this argument following the guidelines covered in APPPENDIX 1:

Conclusion: Donate money to CHEMR instead of to traditional medical charities.

Ambiguity: This argument suffers from some serious ambiguity.

For example, the term "cruel animal experimentation" is not clear. Although Love mentions "starving, freezing, and torturing," we cannot determine why or how such experimentation was done, nor how prevalent it is. We need more detail about this type of experimentation because this is so central to the argument. Dr. Love also argues that "clinical studies involving humans" are more useful than animal experimentation, but does not explain anything about these studies, nor indicate why they are more useful.

Dr. Love suggests that "computer models" have eliminated the need for animal experimentation. What are these computer models? Why are they more effective than animal experimentation?

Finally, Dr. Love states that CHEMR "supports" organizations that do not experiment with animals. What does "supports" mean? Does CHEMR actually donate money to these organizations, or does it just support them in principle? Since the writer is urging us to donate money to CHEMR, we need more detail.

Evidence

The major problem with this argument is that the evidence offered is insufficient to support its conclusion.

Dr. Love argues that nearly $51 million was spent on research, most on animal research. It is likely that the AHA spends a considerable amount of money on research, and the dollar figure would be easy to verify, but the assertion that most of this was spent on animal research is not as obvious, and ogives no support. Furthermore, the contention that the AHA has a history of starving, freezing, and torturing animals is completely unsupported.

Similarly, Dr. Love makes the assertion that the American Cancer Society spends millions of dollars on research, which certainly sounds reasonable, but why should we believe that most of this money goes to fund the type of animal research Dr. Love suggests without more support? Furthermore, to suggest that cancer research involving animals is useless because animal immune systems are different may be an overstatement. Where did this information come from? Similarly, it is an extreme statement to suggest that no new treatment for cancer has been developed through the use of animal experimentation. Considering the many types of cancer treatments being used, this seems highly unlikely, especially with no support.

Dr. Love suggests that computer models have replaced the need for animal testing. Although this may be true, at least in some cases, this claim needs more substantiation. Again, because it is such a broad generalization, it may be difficult to accept without support.

Finally, Dr. Love gives no information about the organizations that CHEMR supports. In fact, this is the only reason that is relevant to CHEMR at all. Dr. Love gives no evidence that CHEMR is an organization worth donating money to. What do they do? Why should we donate to them? The fact that they support organizations that do not experiment on animals is insufficient reason for our support. After all, the American Nazi Party may not conduct animal research, but that, in itself, does not warrant our support.

Assumptions

Dr. Love makes several implicit assumptions that we may question:

1. He apparently assumes that any animal experimentation is, by its very nature, cruel. This may be a value judgment that many readers may share, but it may not be true. Some scientists who experiment with animals may take measures to assure that the animals are being treated in a humane fashion. Although such experimentation may be unpleasant for the animal, it may not necessarily be cruel, so this assumption could be questioned. Some of this research may be done humanely.

2. He assumes that it is only the immune system that determines the usefulness of the research. The immune system is an important body system, but some research might focus more on the respiratory system, or the cardiovascular system, for example, which might not be as affected by the immune system.

3. He is assuming that research money spent by the March of Dimes should show immediate results in preventing birth defects. Presumably, this research often takes years to be effective in lowering birth defects. Therefore, the point about the March of Dimes should be disregarded.

4. The author assumes that computer models will be just as effective as animal experimentation. This may be true in some cases, but it is unlikely to be true in every case. Therefore, this reason is not effective.

Implications

If we accept Dr. Love's reasoning, we will refrain from donating to the American Heart Association, the American Cancer Society, and the March of Dimes. The implications for these organizations would be devastating. Because these organizations rely on private and corporate donations, their work would end or be seriously impaired. These are well-known organizations that have a reputation of doing good work toward the prevention of disease. It is possible that if enough people accepted this argument, more harm would be done than good.

Donating money to CHEMR may be beneficial to reducing animal experimentation. This may be a positive outcome, but at whose expense? And we don't know exactly what CHEMR would do with all the money they'd receive, so we really can't know how much it would help the cause of animal rights.

The implications of this argument are mostly negative.

Bias/Expertise

Certainly, Dr. Love, as a veterinarian, has an informed opinion about animal rights, and probably has some medical knowledge. This enhances his credibility. On the other hand, as executive director of CHEMR, he stands to gain from donations to that organization. So he certainly has a bias, which may be affecting his judgment.

Improvements

The single biggest improvement to this argument would be to provide more detail about how animal experimentation is both *unnecessary* and *cruel*. Both of these assertions are essential to the argument, and neither one has sufficient evidence backing it up. If more examples could be given, with the sources listed, to verify that these organizations conduct cruel experiments on animals, he would have a much better case. It would also be helpful to provide some testimony or other evidence to support his contention that computer models have made animal experimentation unnecessary.

Dr. Love should have also provided more direct evidence about how these organizations spend their money. He needs to make a case that this money is not well spent. We need to know how they DO spend their money if we are to stop donating to them.

Finally, Dr. Love provides no information about CHEMR. How are we to know whether we should donate to an organization if we do not know what its purpose is or what, exactly, it will do with the money?

Overall, this is a weak argument with little substantive evidence to back up its conclusion.

A Gentle Way to Die
Katie Letcher Lyle
Newsweek, March 2, 1992.
(Used with permission)

The stripes of gold, khaki and black melted into each other until I blinked back the tears. If we did nothing, Gov might last another painful month. Everything medical that could be done had been done. So I made the decision, recalling the day we brought the kitten to our then-new house. For 16 years we enjoyed Gov's beautiful presence in our laps, in sun squares, by fires, on windowsills where he conversed with bluejays, on the kitchen counter kibitzing for a scrap or following raptly the stuffing of a turkey. He poked curiously about each new baby as we brought it home. "Govie Lovie" our daughter, younger than he by half, called him.

But he grew old. With cancer of his spine, maybe elsewhere, he was no longer interested in food and his bladder and bowels were embarrassingly out of control. Sadly I watched the doctor shave his thin forearm, stroked his soft, vibrating side, as the needle was prepared. Gov didn't even flinch when it slid in. About five seconds, the gold eyes glazed, then half closed and the purr stopped. No pain.

I think about Gov sometimes when I visit a beloved, ancient friend, her mind absolutely gone for six years, her body ticking on relentlessly, her round-the-clock nurses dressing her like a doll. Fritchie never speaks, reacts hardly at all, never opens her eyes. But she must exist in some unimaginable hell, for tears often squeeze out between her eyelids. I wish her the swift merciful death we gave our pet, but probably she will go on until recurring cancer kills her slowly, cruelly.

Now here is the difficult case. Today I attended a meeting in another state about a man whom I represent. Consider Henry, 40, six feet tall, strong, affectionate, loves action movies, his IQ in the profoundly retarded range. He used to pick up trash at a parking lot, until the manager's patience wore too thin. He can unload restaurant dishes from tray to sink-- but only with constant supervision and encouragement.

Henry was abandoned to the state in infancy by parents who are affluent professionals whom I don't know and whose other children don't know about Henry. Shunted from place to place, Henry now lives in a 10-man group home where, for months, he functioned adequately.

But recently, things have gone badly. He has, after countless last chances, been fired. Consistency is extremely important to Henry, but new employers don't understand that, and there's rapid turnover in the restaurant business. In the day care program where he is now, Henry's unpredictable outbursts have injured staff members and another client, and terrified clients and staff.

At home, he has destroyed much of the furniture, and intimidated every other resident with his towering tantrums. The other clients spend their free time in their rooms while

Henry watches TV alone. His strength overpowers the home's help and during "time out," he destroys everything around him. Outings, parties, ball games are rewards for good behavior. So recently, Henry has been excluded from the good times. He's encouraged to hit pillows with Styrofoam bats. But when he's mad, he wants to hit whomever he's mad at. Extensive medical and neurological tests reveal no health problems, no seizures. Endless psychological investigations suggest what's already been tried: behavior modification, Tranxene.

He has been told often that he cannot stay in his home if these outbursts continue-- but does he understand? What is home if not where you live? The destructive behavior is escalating, becoming more violent, occurring more often, 13 major episodes last month. Staff members are afraid. One's already resigned.

At our meeting to consider what to do next, Henry "writes" on a yellow tablet, a self-calming technique he has learned, and as usual seems almost normal, nodding and looking at people who are speaking. On his table are line after line of scribble. He interrupts to whine that it's cold, but it's not, and he has on a heavy sweater. He interrupts continually, and at one point simply begins to cry, loudly, his face and eyes red, real tears.

He is told he will have to leave if he doesn't stop howling. But the social workers insist on his presence, because of his "client's rights," and because he "needs to be involved as much as possible." The wailing ebbs, but now Henry babbles about his birthday party. The facility where he lived before cannot take him back; his place has been filled. The house were he's living has a long waiting list of eligible clients.

The next step, if he continues to make life unlivable for the other clients and staff, is removal, probably to an overcrowded state institution facing brutal budget cuts. Every door is closing; there seems to be nowhere else for him to go.

I know the arguments about the abuses of kindly death, and I know mental incompetents were the Nazi's first victims. The money is certainly not the point; I believe strongly that one can judge any civilization by how decently it treats its sick, its elderly, its disabled. But money is a reality, and adding up all the institutional, medical and social services, Henry has already cost American taxpayers $1.5 million. But my point is, what does *life* hold for Henry now? I'll tell you: either a drugged hell of an existence behind bars; or, more probably, deinstitutionalization, street life, an agonizing death in a filthy alley. It happens to others, everywhere, every day.

I don't like the conclusion I'm forced to. But is a gentle death for a human being always the worst answer? Laws can be implemented to prevent abuses. It seems patently untrue that *any life* is always preferable to *no life*. I wish, more than I can say, that there is someplace on this earth where Henry could live happily and freely and be loved and understood. But since there isn't, I find it disgraceful, as well as ironic, that we cannot bring ourselves to treat our fellow human beings as humanely as we treat our pets.

Lyle, a freelance writer, is actively involved as a volunteer on three boards advocating on behalf of the handicapped.

The following is a good example of a commentary which that be prepared for this argument following the guidelines covered in APPENDIX I:

Conclusion: As a society, we should seriously consider euthanasia for people with serious disabilities or illnesses.

Ambiguity

Lyle's proposal is fairly unambiguous. She seems to be suggesting that we put suffering humans to death the same way we do with suffering animals. The reasons are fairly unambiguous. There is, however, some serious ambiguity in her main example: the case of Henry.

Lyle mentions that Henry has "unpredictable outbursts," yet the specific nature of these outbursts is not clear. She suggests they are violent, but we do not know exactly what they consist of.

She suggests that he has undergone "extensive psychological investigations," but how extensive have they been? We need to know this before we can accept her premise that nothing more can be done for Henry. This ambiguity is central to her conclusion.

Lyle introduces further ambiguity in her description of what Henry's options are, "either a drugged hell of an existence behind bars or, more probably, deinstitutionalization, street life, an agonizing death in a filthy alley." She does not elaborate on this assessment. She asks us to accept it without further detail. We need to know why she concludes this in order to determine whether she is correct in her assessment of Henry's situation.

Evidence

Lyle offers the information about her pet as typical. This is reasonable evidence and does not require additional information. Most pet owners can identify with the scenario she describes.

She also offers information about her aging friend, Fritchie. We are given Lyle's impressions of Fritchie's condition, but we are offered no clear medical information about her. We'd need more evidence to assess her overall condition, especially to accept Lyle's ultimate solution.

Lyle offers evidence about Henry's situation, but we cannot easily determine whether or not his situation really warrants the drastic solution she is suggesting. For example, she argues that nothing more can be done for Henry, that his options have been reduced to two, either one of which will not provide any kind of happy life for Henry. I am left wondering whether Henry's psychiatrists or other mental health professionals agree with Lyle's bleak assessment. It would seem to me that someone who can function at this high a level would have some more reasonable options. She offers no strong evidence for her assessments.

To accept her conclusion, we'd at least need to have significantly more information about Henry, including the opinions of other professionals. We also would need to know how typical Henry's case is.

If we are going to accept her conclusion that Henry be put to death, then we are going to need to know how such a program can be carried out in a way that would prevent abuses. Lyle states, "Laws can be implemented to prevent abuses." What kinds of laws? Have such laws been tried in any other countries? Why does she think these laws would work?

Assumptions

Lyle makes a number of questionable implicit assumptions:

1. She assumes that Henry's life is not worth living in its present state and that he will never attain a better quality of life. Determining what an appropriate quality of life is for someone else is not easy. Although it may appear his life is not worth living, I don't believe we can know this. And we certainly can't know what his quality of life might be in the future with better treatment.

2. She assumes that $1.5 million is an unreasonable amount to spend on Henry. This is, of course, a value judgment. It is a lot of money, but if the outcome could be a positive one for Henry, it may not be foolishly spent. How do we put a value on human life? She suggests that money is not the point, but then points out that, in this case, it may be.

3. She assumes that her assessment of Henry's options is correct: that he will live in a drugged stupor or die painfully on the street. This appears to be an oversimplification. Rarely are there only two options. Perhaps other professionals might disagree with this assessment.

4. She assumes that Henry's situation is comparable to Fritchie's. It appears to me that Fritchie, suffering form a devastating physical illness, has fewer options than Henry. Perhaps she'd make a better case for involuntary euthanasia by focusing more on cases like Fritchie's.

Implications

The most troubling aspects of Lyle's argument are the implications of her reasoning. If we accept the idea that involuntary euthanasia could be accepted, then we, as a society, would obviously have to come up with a system to manage the details. Who, for example, would decide who should be euthanized? How would they decide? How would the euthanasia be conducted? How would safeguards be put into place? These are not easy questions to answer, but they must be addressed before we could seriously consider such a proposal.

Another implication of her reasoning is that this could be abused. Families could ask to have their relatives euthanized for financial or convenience reasons.

A positive implication of her reasoning is that money could be saved for the taxpayers. This is clearly true, since all cost of care would end with the client's death.

Another positive implication is that the suffering of patients like Henry would be eliminated. We see many homeless, mentally ill people on the streets today. If they were euthanized, we would see fewer people suffering like this.

Bias/Expertise

Lyle does have some experience working with the handicapped, and acts as an advocate for them. She obviously cares what happens to them. She is a freelance writer who may not be an expert in the mental health field. Some bias might creep into her reasoning because of her work with these clients. She might feel so hopeless and empathetic about their plight that she might see this as a way to deal with the emotional pain of seeing these people suffer. Her emotional pain may be influencing her perspective.

Improvements

It appears that it will be difficult to construct a good argument to support her conclusion, because her conclusion is so drastic. She is suggesting that we put people to death without their permission. It seems that she'd have a better case for this with Fritchie than with Henry. Fritchie is obviously not going to get better, and it seems clearer that her quality of life is questionable. Henry's life, on the other hand, is more complex. It is not clear that Henry's life could not be improved in some way. So she should probably use more examples like Fritchie to make her case, and eliminate Henry's case altogether. His case hurts her conclusion more than it helps.

If she wants to keep Henry's case as part of her argument, we need lots more evidence. We need to hear from some mental health professionals about Henry's prognosis. We need to have more information about what they think Henry's options are. We need to know, in other words, how accurate her assessment is.

Since she is arguing for involuntary euthanasia, it would be helpful to know about other countries, like the Netherlands, which have laws allowing this type of thing.

What types of guidelines do they have? What problems are they having? If it is working well in other countries, that would support allowing such a practice in the United States.

Overall, it's easy to see why Lyle would favor such an idea, but it is very drastic and would be difficult to sell without a lot more evidence.

APPENDIX IV
Arguments for Analysis

Paying for Organs Would Save Lives
Boston Sunday Globe, Oct.12, 2003
Jeff Jacoby
(Used with permission)

For a classic illustration of the Law of Unintended Consequences, consider the National Organ Transplant Act.

Passed by Congress in 1984, the statute makes it illegal to pay any compensation to organ donors or their families. The lawmakers' intentions were good: They were loath to allow the spectacle of human organs being bought and sold like mere commodities. And they wanted to prevent any chance that the poor would be exploited to supply body parts for the rich.

Those things have indeed been prevented. But by making it a crime to offer donors any "valuable consideration" for organs, Congress achieved something else too: the unnecessary deaths of tens of thousands of Americans who could have been saved if only the organs they needed had been available.

The problem with the system Congress created is that it relies on altruism alone to stimulate organ donations. That isn't enough, as the rising death toll makes agonizingly clear. Some 80,000 people are waiting for an organ transplant right now; another 3,000 patients are added to the waiting list each month. But in 2002, only 24,900 organs were available for transplantation, and more than 6,500 patients died while awaiting an organ that never came.

The number of organs being supplied by living donors-- usually kidneys being given to a relative-- has been growing, from fewer than 2,000 in 1989 to nearly 6,000 now. But most vital organs are obtained from donors, who have just died, and the number of these cadaveric donations, as they are called, has hardly budged in recent years. Between 15,000 and 20,000 decedents annually meet the physical criteria for cadaveric donation, but only about 35 percent of the time do their families give permission for organs to be removed.

Would more families be willing to give that permission-- and would more Americans sign up to be organ donors-- if they were offered a financial incentive to do so? Sure they would. The best way to end almost any shortage is to boost supply by raising the price. Donor families are currently offered nothing to make a dead relative's organs available. It isn't surprising that so many say no. Make them a better offer, and more will say yes.

Some advocates have been making this argument for years, urging an amendment to the 1984 law that would permit the families of cadaveric donors to be compensated. As Carey Goldberg reported last week in The Boston Globe, Pennsylvania congressman James Greenwood had introduced a bill to do just that. The American Medical Association used to oppose financial incentives for organ donations; now it says the "time has come" to give them a serious test. Its call has been endorsed by two key institutional players, the American Society of Transplant Surgeons and the United Network for Organ Sharing.

So what would an organ-donor incentive look like? Proposals vary. Three years ago, Pennsylvania's Legislature voted to pay $300 toward the funeral expenses of families that donated a deceased loved one's organs. It was never implemented because of the conflict with the 1984 federal law, but at the time, essayist (and MD) Charles Krauthammer pronounced the bill "too timid." Instead of giving the money to funeral homes, he asked; why not pay the families directly? "And why not $3000 instead of $300? After all, $3000 is real money, even for bankers and lawyers."

Richard Devos, a founder of the Amway Corp., goes further. He recommends letting insurance companies pay a $10,000 benefit to the designated beneficiary of anyone who agrees to donate his organs, should the donor become brain-dead through accident or illness. Why would insurance companies want such a plan? Because it costs far less to transplant an organ than to provide indefinite treatment for a patient on the waiting list. For example, insurance companies save as much as $400,000 every time a donated kidney frees a patient from dialysis.

At the other end of the financial scale is a proposal by Donald Boudreaux and Adam Pritchard, adjunct scholars with Mackinac Center in Michigan. Their idea is to offer a very small payment, no more than $25, to anyone who agrees to donate his organs after death. That small incentive, they predict, would induce thousands of healthy people to sign donor registries. The fee would be paid not by the government but by a nonprofit organization like the Red Cross. In return, whenever a hospital or insurer used a donated organ, it would make a large reimbursement payment to the nonprofit.

Anything that smacks of "commercializing" human organs is sure to provoke criticism, of course. And rightly so, perhaps, if the issue were how to boost organ donations from live donors. But the old taboo against paying for organs even from the dead cannot be allowed to stand. Not when 6,500 people a year are losing their lives because of it. Congress made a lethal mistake in 1984. The sooner it rectifies it, the sooner the dying will stop.

Try Something Different for Weak Students
USA Today, April 15, 2002
John Merrow
(Used with permission)

New York City's school board is deeply divided over whether to make drastic cuts in its summer school program. Last year, 269,620 students in grades 3 through 12 attended summer school at a cost of $176 million. If any cuts are made, however, it will be to save money, not because of a loss of faith in the idea of summer school.

"If you can provide kids with extra time," said school board member Terri Thomson of summer school, "they improve."

Actually, I don't think the kind of "extra time" now offered matters a bit.

Summer school, in New York and elsewhere, is little more than mindless repetition of failed practices. Yet summer school is being mandated in a growing number of public systems around the country.

Chicago started the trend in the late 1990s, but the roster of cities mandating summer school for students who haven't met the new education standards now includes Miami-Dade; Oakland; Long Beach; Greenville, S.C.; Baton Rouge; Richmond, VA.; Dallas; Davenport, Iowa; Oxnard, California; and Orange City, Florida, among others.

The growth in summer schooling is a response to the demand for an end to what is called "social promotion," the practice of keeping students with their age peers regardless of their academic performance. Social promotion is based on the belief that making a struggling child repeat a grade does more harm than good. But it conjures up powerful images of students being passed along even though they can't pass tests, write coherent sentences or read.

Most Americans believe that social promotion is wrong. It's also something politicians of varied persuasions are against. Bill Clinton, George W. Bush, and New York Mayor Michael Bloomberg have opposed it and campaigned to end it.

Now many school districts have replaced social promotion with "retention" -- what most of us call "staying back." Unfortunately, ending social promotion has not yet solved the underlying problem of school failure-- and summer school in its current form doesn't help, either.

What happens to students who are retained? What opportunities does the system provide to enable students to catch up? Normally, it's summer school and more of the same. That is, most remediation programs are echoes of what already has failed.

Think of it this way: Imagine you are driving into town, looking for the Wal-Mart. You get lost and ask me for directions. I tell you how many blocks to go, when to turn left, and so on, but you do not understand. (If you are with me on this, you are the student, and I'm the teacher.)

When I realize that you are confused, I simply repeat the directions, only this time I SHOUT. It won't take you long to realize that you never will get where you want to go with me as your guide, so you step on the gas and seek help elsewhere.

That's a pretty fair description of how schools treat failure. First of all, just as I blamed you for not grasping my directions, it's the student's fault for not understanding. Summer school is the equivalent of my shouting the same words. So just as you would give up on me and drive away, many students who are retained drop out of school.

At a time when President Bush talks about leaving no child behind, teachers need to find more creative ways to remediate these students.

The Bush administration believes that testing students every year will end the problem, because failure will be spotted early. In that sense, it is right, but if schools don't provide thoughtful -- and different -- remediation programs, nothing important will change, and kids will continue to pay the price of our failure.

So how do we fix it?

Get back in your car for a minute and I will tell you. First of all, I wouldn't shout at you, because I would want you to get to your destination. I would try new approaches; find different ways to explain my directions, until you felt ready to go on down the road. That is, I would feel that I had failed (as your teacher) if I couldn't help you get where you were going.

So, to be successful, summer school teachers should begin by abandoning what has not worked and adopt a new motto: "If students don't learn, then we have not taught."

Change the location, schedule field trips and overnight excursions, put kids in groups, teach in teams, and experiment with technology. I recall a summer-reading program that took advantage of the students' obsession with basketball. They had one rule: Only those who had done the reading may suit up. Then, about a dozen times during the games, the ref would blow his whistle for vocabulary words. If you could define the word, your team got one point, but if you could not, someone for the other team got the opportunity to score. "Vocabulary points" decided most games, and, believe me, that worked.

Of course, students and teachers and schools must be held accountable for falling short, but the goal of schooling ought to be learning, not simply doing a better job of placing the blame.

That means discarding what isn't working.

No more shouting!